"There are often strong about, things that hold u Christ. Whether we have these things, if not dealt with, allow open doors for the enemy to enter and torment us in one way or another. The instructions in this book will allow you to be totally set free from what cycles you back into sin, depression, and weakness. It will teach you how to be set free and stay free. Time is valuable. It is my honor and privilege to recommend this book for you to spend some of that time investing in yourself and the Kingdom of God."

—*Sandra Hardister Querin, JD, MBA, ThD., pastor, The Revival Center, Clovis, California, and author,* The Prayer of Moses, The Prayer of Job, and The Dynamics of Spiritual Warfare

"Caryn's book is a powerful tool for shutting down the enemy's plan to keep you in bondage. Discover the keys that not only close open doors but lock them shut, bringing true freedom. Powerful, amazing, and life changing, *Open Doors* is a must read for all Christians."

—*Lauren Sloan, Leader of Moms of Encouragement*

"Anyone who has been a Christian even for a short time knows that you can be born again and love God and still struggle in areas of your life. This can be true both for new Christians and for those saved for decades. God's promises, such as having peace, often elude us, and we don't know why. A common reason is that there are spiritual truths or laws that are affecting us even if we're not aware of it— just like gravity affects you whether you understand it or not. Caryn's book on *Open Doors* to the enemy and how they give him access to our lives explains these critical truths. You can love the Lord and do your best, and yet be forever frustrated because the enemy keeps getting in. I highly recommend this book for every Christian. It will help you so that you can better help others. Shutting every door to the enemy is easy and will have a huge impact on your life!"

—*Doug Mosemann, MS, Strategic Account Manager to Fortune 500 Companies*

"Goodbye Open Doors! Sayonara Habitual Sins! Ever feel like you're in a rocking chair, rocking faster than the speed of light but not going anywhere? Ever consider those cords tying you down just may be stretched through your own Open Doors? The words of these pages are a culmination of Caryn Kilgore's life journey: listening to the wisdom of God, pulling out and destroying strongholds, and severing the cords that tie saints down. Open Doors are avenues by which the enemy takes his foothold. Now it's up to you to take a deep dive into these pages and discover what doors have remained open; ...the doors causing havoc in your Christian walk. You will learn how to slam those doors shut, keep them shut, and maintain a victorious lifestyle in Christ. Begin your sustainable recovery here and now."
—*Samuel Sullivan, F/A-18 Quality Assurance Specialist*

"*Open Doors* is a terrific guide to getting yourself free from the grip of the enemy. So often we struggle with sin because we don't have the understanding of what we have actually opened ourselves to in the past. Not only does Caryn Kilgore explain the various types of doors and how to shut them, but she also gives many wonderful helps in how to remain an overcomer once those doors are shut! Whether you are growing in your pursuit of God or just beginning, understanding the principles and guidelines in *Open Doors* is a must for every believer. I highly recommend this book!"
—*Vivien Cooley, teacher and author*

"*Open Doors* is easy reading, exposing deep truths for identifying the open doors of the enemy and breaking strongholds with practical application on how to close those doors. Having the privilege of working with Caryn for 30 years, I have witnessed countless people break the strongholds, close the enemy's doors, and be set free by applying these fundamental and yet powerful truths found in God's Word."
—*Pamela Luper, CFO and owner of WML Safeguard Protection and Consulting, Inc.*

"Caryn Kilgore is a wonderful example of how to implement these steps in our lives, and how they will work to mold us into the image of Jesus. Not only has she lived these steps out in her own life, but she, through her years of counseling, has witnessed this transformation in the lives of others who have had the same conviction to follow God's ways and seek His wholeness and healing. I would encourage anyone who desires to be truly free to start with Jesus, and to exercise the steps in this book, *Open Doors*, as a guide to closing the open doors in their lives that would otherwise hinder them fully seeking His face. I pray for you all to find Jesus and let Him transform you through His presence and His Word."

—*Samantha Glenn, homemaker and artist*

"God has given Caryn insight on *Open Doors* that hold His people back and how to keep those doors closed. I have seen many repent and close doors and have the peace of God come over them. It has changed their lives and these principles have helped many people walk closer to the Lord. Very beautiful."

—*Lori Snow, biblical counselor*

"This book will transform lives, teach how to break strongholds, overcome obstacles, close doors, stand against the enemy, and learn how to walk in the true power of our Lord Jesus Christ! I have had the honor to know Caryn for the past 20 years and have seen lives changed and people be victorious as they follow these Bible-based truths found in her book, *Open Doors*."

—*Dora Harris, ministry events coordinator*

Open Doors

The Keys to Overcoming and Living Free

Caryn Ann Kilgore

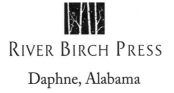

RIVER BIRCH PRESS

Daphne, Alabama

ISBN 978-1-951561-76-5 (print)
ISBN 978-1-951561-77-2 (e-book)
For Worldwide Distribution
Printed in the U.S.A.

River Birch Press
P.O. Box 868, Daphne, AL 36526

Contents

I LIFT MY EYES TO THE
mountains
WHERE DOES MY
help come from?
MY HELP COMES FROM
the Lord
MAKER OF
heaven & earth
PSALM 121

Foreword

What you hold in your hand is a Freedom Manual. Upon reading this book and applying its principles, you will not only go beyond wounds and the terrors of your life; but you will learn how to get through recovery and abide in the "land of the living" as Psalm 27:13 declares. In just a few days from now, you will have positioned yourself to dwell in that land as a constant overcomer.

I have known these principles to be life changing for myself and countless others who have submitted to the process. This is a book that does not celebrate recovery... it gets you beyond recovery and celebrates an abundant life in Christ as a sanctified vessel who is NOT going backwards, but rather taking ground for Jesus Christ and saving the world for His glory.

Often, there are strongholds in our lives, things we do not know about, things that hold us back from living a solid and true life in Christ. Whether we have known Christ for 5 minutes or 50 years, these things, if not dealt with, allow "open doors" for the enemy to enter and torment us in one way or another. The instructions in this book will allow you to be totally set free from what cycles you back into sin, depression and weakness.

Caryn Kilgore has been teaching these principles for 30 years as a Bible teacher and Biblical counsellor. She is active in her church, The Revival Center in Clovis, California, as a discipleship trainer, teacher, leader, Intercessor and key staff member. I have known her for 25 years and consider her a choice vessel of God.

Time is valuable. It is my honor and privilege to recommend this book for you to spend some of that time investing in yourself and the Kingdom of God.

Jesus said, In the world you will have tribulation. But, be of good cheer, for I have overcome the world (John 16:33).

In the bonds of Calvary with hope and love,
Sandra Hardister Querin, JD, MBA, ThD., pastor, The Revival Center, Clovis, California; author, *The Prayer of Moses*, *The Prayer of Job*, and *The Dynamics of Spiritual Warfare*

Trust in the LORD
with all your heart
and do not lean on
your own understanding.
In all your ways
acknowledge Him
and He will make straight
your paths.

Proverbs 3:5-6

Introduction

In over 25 years of doing biblical counseling, I have encountered many problems. The majority of these problems have stemmed from open doors. Many years ago, while discipling new believers, I became concerned about those who would continuously fall back into sin after accepting the Lord. I asked the Lord about this and here is the answer He gave me: "They have open doors in their life." The open door(s) gave the enemy the legal right to access and torment them.

When we were following our own sinful natures and not following the Lord, we sinned and these sins opened a spiritual door(s) to the enemy. It gave the enemy, the devil, a legal right to access, accuse, and torment us. The enemy needs only one open door in a believer's life to gain a foothold. Unfortunately, many of us have more than one open door in our lives.

These sins need to be overcome, and the doors that were opened by these sins need to be closed. It is much easier to overcome that sin when the door to that sin is closed. When you close an open door, it makes you aware that you are in charge of your actions. An open door does not negate your salvation but it does keep you from living an overcoming life.

I discovered that there are four areas of open doors: generational sins, sexual immorality, drugs and addiction, and occult and false religion. In this book I will share with you how to close those doors and give you the keys to living free in your own life.

After you have closed the open doors in your life, learn the keys to living free, and how to keep these doors to the enemy closed by guarding your heart, renewing your mind, and retraining your brain. You will discover the roots and strongholds that unfortunately we all have in our lives, how to pull them out, replacing them instead with godly attributes.

As we walk out our faith, what do we need to watch out for?

How do we keep the enemy from hindering our walk with the Lord? Learn how to hear the voice of the Lord, persevere in your faith, prefer Him, and run your race to make a difference for the Kingdom of God!

To my loving husband, Allen.

I could not be all that the Lord

has called me to be without

your love, support, and encouragement.

The Lord has greatly blessed me

by giving me you, our children,

and grandchildren.

Four Areas of Open Doors

Generational Sins

Sexual Immorality

Drugs and Addiction

The Occult and False Religion

⌐1⌐

WHAT ARE OPEN DOORS?

For this is the love of God, that we keep His commandments, and His commandments are not burdensome. For everyone who has been born of God overcomes the world. And this is the victory that has overcome the world—our faith (1 John 5:3-4 ESV).

Have you become a Christian and yet continue to struggle to overcome sinful habits? This book will give you the key to living an overcoming life for the Lord. This key is *Open Doors*.

Open doors have been around since the inception of sin. In the garden, Adam and Eve chose to listen to the enemy, disobey God, and sin. Their sin opened a door to the enemy (see Genesis 3:1-13).

I will share with you principles I teach every person that I counsel and every new believer. I wish I had known them in my teenage years so I could have avoided open doors in my own life. I also wish someone would have taught them to me when I was a young Christian. In school they teach children to "Say no to drugs," which is well and good, but that is just one door. In this book I will teach you about all four open doors and how to close them.

When we become a Christian and receive Jesus Christ as our Lord and Savior, we need to close some spiritual doors. You may ask, but when I accepted Jesus as my Savior, weren't my sins forgiven? Yes, they were!

First John 1:9 says: *If we confess our sins, He is faithful and just to forgive us our sins and to cleanse us from all unrighteousness.*

1

The blood of Jesus wiped away our sins, and we are forgiven. We have an eternity in heaven to look forward to with the Lord, and our name is written down in the Book of Life. Unfortunately, all of the habits and sinful patterns formed by these sins do not automatically disappear.

These sins need to be overcome, and the doors that were opened by these sins need to be closed. It is much easier to overcome a sin when the door to that sin is closed. When you close an open door, it makes you aware that you are in charge of your actions. An open door does not negate your salvation, but it does keep you from living an overcoming life. Romans 3:23 says: *All have sinned and fallen short of the glory of God.*

When we were following our own sinful natures and not following the Lord, we sinned and these sins opened a spiritual door(s) to the enemy. It gave the enemy, the devil, a legal right to access, accuse, and torment you. The enemy needs only one open door in the believer's life to gain a foothold. Unfortunately, many of us have more than one open door.

It is important to realize that our sins are not just sin, but they have actually opened a door to the enemy. How many of us would think twice about committing that sin if we knew this?

Many of us know someone who has used drugs and then became a Christian. They really want to follow the Lord and become a disciple of His, but the draw of the drugs keeps pulling them back into that lifestyle. That is an open door of drugs. They need to cut off the enemy's legal right to access and torment them through that open door. By closing the door to drugs, they can move forward and live an overcoming life, reaching their best potential.

An open door is basically a sin. It is a metaphor for opening yourself to a particular sin. How does sin start? With a thought. Then you entertain it, and then act upon it. The root of sin is pride and our own self-centered sinful desires, our sinful nature.

But each one is tempted when by his own evil desire, he is dragged away and enticed. Then after desire has conceived, it gives birth to sin; and sin, when it is full grown, gives birth to death (James 1:14-15).

Some of the doors you may have opened yourself and others may have been opened by your parents or grandparents. These are generational sins.

Four Areas of Open Doors:

1. Generational Sins
2. Sexual Immorality
3. Drugs and Addiction
4. The Occult and False Religion

As you learn about these doors and what doors you have opened in your life, you will learn how to close them. You will also learn how to pull out the roots and strongholds that have grown and developed in your life; the importance of guarding your heart, renewing your mind, retraining your brain, and walking it out; how to overcome sin with scripture; and your authority in Christ. Then you will truly be on your way to living an overcoming life.

In today's world, many things beckon to us that say this is the way, such as New Age beliefs, false religion, idolatry (putting anything in the place of God), atheism, and even our own sinful nature.

Jesus said: I am the way, and the truth, and the life. No one can come to the Father except through me (John 14:6 ESV).

There is only one true way to God and that is through His Son, Jesus Christ. You can know about God yet not know God. He wants to have a personal relationship with you through His Son, Jesus Christ.

The most important decision you can ever make is to invite Jesus into your heart to be your Lord and Savior. That is why I am beginning this book talking about this subject. The following are the steps to find peace with God and to accept Jesus as your Lord and Savior:

God Has a Plan for You and Your Life.

God loves you and wants you to experience His wonderful peace and life.

For God so loved the world that He gave His only begotten Son, that whoever believes in Him should not perish but have everlasting life. For God did not send His Son into the world to condemn the world, but to save the world through Him (John 3:16-17).

Our Problem Is We Are Separated from God.

Our sin creates a barrier between us and God.

For all have sinned and fall short of the glory of God (Romans 3:23).

God's Remedy - The Cross of Jesus Christ

God's love bridges the gap of separation between God and us. When His Son Jesus Christ died on the cross and rose from the grave, He paid the penalty for our sins. The cross of Jesus Christ is the bridge. That bridge creates the pathway for us to be able to cross over from our sin to new life with the Lord.

He personally carried the load of our sins in his own body when he died on the cross (1 Peter 2:24).

Our Decision Is to Receive Jesus Christ.

Yet, to all who received Him, to those who believed in His name, He gave the right to become children of God (John 1:12).

To receive Jesus as your Lord and Savior you need to do three things:

1. **Accept** Jesus as your personal Savior.
2. **Believe** that Jesus is the Son of God, and that He died for you, and your sins on the Cross, then rose again.
3. **Confess** your sins, and ask Jesus to forgive you, and to come into your heart and life.

If we claim to be without sin, we deceive ourselves and the truth is not in us. If we confess our sins, He is faithful and just and will forgive us our sins and purify us from all unrighteousness (1 John 1:8-9).

For the wages of sin is death, but the gift of God is eternal life in Christ Jesus our Lord (Romans 6:23).

If you declare with your mouth, "Jesus is Lord" and believe in your heart that God raised him from the dead, you will be saved (Romans 10:9).

Whoever calls upon the name of the Lord will be saved (Romans 10:13).

This prayer is for salvation to invite Jesus into your heart. Chapter 6 has the closing doors prayer.

What to Pray:

Dear Lord Jesus, I know that I am a sinner and I ask you to forgive me for my sins. I believe that You are the Son of God and You died on the Cross for my sins then rose from the dead. I want to turn from my sins. I invite You to come into my heart and life. I want to trust and follow You as my Lord and Savior. In Jesus name, Amen.

Therefore, God exalted Him to the highest place and gave Him the name that is above every name, that at the name of Jesus every knee should bow, in heaven and on earth and under the earth, and every tongue acknowledge that Jesus Christ is Lord, to the glory of God the Father (Philippians 2:9-11).

Now that you have asked Jesus into your heart, the next step is to make Him Lord of your life.

Lordship

Jesus said in Luke 9:23-24: *If anyone would come after me, he must deny himself and take up his cross daily and follow me. For whoever wants to save his life will lose it, but whoever loses his life for me will save it.*

I'm going to share with you the principle of Lordship, making Jesus Lord of your life. Lordship is praying and asking Jesus Christ to take control of your life through the Holy Spirit. It is turning complete control of your life over to Jesus. It is not just an outward profession but an inward sincere desire and attitude of your heart.

Let's use driving as an example. When we first experience salvation, it is like inviting Jesus into our car in the passenger seat. We are still in control. We are still driving. But that doesn't work out very well! Lordship is letting Jesus drive and take control of our lives. When we yield control of our lives to Him, the drive goes so much better that way!

Jesus is specifically called "Savior" sixteen times in the New Testament and "Lord" more than four hundred and fifty times. Lord means: having power, dominion, authority, and the right to master. We cannot submit to Christ's Lordship without submitting to God's Word. Receiving Jesus as Savior but not making Him Lord of your life will not result in a lasting salvation.

Making Jesus truly Lord of your life will allow you to walk in fellowship with Him. He will become your best friend. A wonderful example of Lordship is the booklet: *My Heart—Christ's Home* by Robert Boyd Munger. I encourage you to read this booklet. Make Jesus Lord of your life and over every part of your heart.

I pray that from His glorious, unlimited resources He will empower you with inner strength through His Spirit. Then Christ will make His home in your hearts as you trust in Him. Your roots will grow down into God's love and keep you strong (Ephesians 3:16-17 NLT).

Scriptures on Lordship: Psalm 37:4-5; Mark 12:30; Luke 9:23-24; John 14:23, 15:11; Acts 2:36-40, 8:16, 19:5; Romans 8:39, 10:9-10, 10:13; 1 Corinthians 12:3; Ephesians 3:16-17; Revelation 3:20.

AS FOR ME AND MY

house

WE WILL SERVE

The Lord

JOSHUA 24:15

THE OPEN DOOR OF GENERATIONAL SINS

Generational sins are sins that are prevalent in your family line that your parents and grandparents participated in or allowed in their bloodline. Generational sins are a result of doors that were opened before you and thus predisposed you to those sins. A generational sin(s) can lead to an open door in that area and can also lead you to opening that door in your own life and participating in that sin. These sins often are passed down time and time again to the next generation.

I have observed that many of us have open doors in this area. The good news is that the Lord can redeem that. He can close those doors so that moving forward they will not affect you, your children, or grandchildren again.

> **Generational Sins:** *Including, but not limited to* Alcoholism, Drug Addiction, Substance Abuse, Anger, Lying, Prejudice, Hatred, Judgement, Rebellion, Stealing, Perversion, Immorality, Incest, Adultery, Molestation, Pornography, Witchcraft, Voodoo, the Occult, Secret Orders, Masons, Rainbow Girls, De Molay, Job's Daughters, Gangs, Cleansings, Violence, Gambling, Fear, Cults, False Religion, New Age.

Those who went before you participated in these sins. You may or may not have participated in them, but due to the generations before you opening that door(s), it does affect you and your family line. To live an overcoming life, these door(s) of generational sins must be closed.

One family I know had three generations of molestation that I knew about. It could possibly have gone on for much longer. Most likely the abuser was also sexually abused as a child. These "secret" sins cause so much damage. But through the blood of Jesus and closing that open doorway, the generational sin is broken and will not continue forward.

It does not seem fair that sins in which we did not even participate must be repented of and broken. This is because these are generational open doors.

Look at these scriptures:

Choose for yourselves this day whom your will serve, whether the gods which your fathers served that were on the other side of the river, or the gods of the Amorites, in whose land you dwell. But as for me and my house, we will serve the Lord (Joshua 24:15).

You shall not make for yourself a carved image, any likeness of anything that is in heaven above, or that is in the earth beneath, or that is in the water under the earth; you shall not bow down and serve them. For I, The Lord Your God, am a jealous God, visiting the iniquity of the fathers upon the children to the third and fourth generations of those who hate me, but showing mercy to thousands, to those who love me and keep my commandments (Exodus 20:4-6).

I'm sure we can all think of at least one family we know with generational evidence of open door sins being passed down to the next generation.

In counseling I have learned that when a person tells me they have dealt with feelings of wanting to commit suicide, I need to ask if they ever had a relative or person they know do a "cleansing" on them. More often than not, the spirit of suicide came in then. When the relative performed a ritual of cleaning out the bad spirits, in reality they were performing a demonic ritual and placing a bad spirit, such as the spirit of suicide or other bad spirits in them. This is very prevalent and common in some cultures.

We know that alcoholism and drug addiction are many times passed down from one generation to another. Why? These behaviors (sins) are open doors and children learn what they live. This is especially true of families where there is abuse and anger. The parents have modeled the anger and abuse for the children whether it be verbal or physical.

One young woman I counseled had a grandmother who practiced witchcraft and cleansings. There were also generations of physical molestation that had been kept secret and never brought out into the open. This led those in the family to bear the repercussions of the generational sins with the evidences of sexual immorality, molestation, incest, abuse, an affinity towards the occult, mental illness, and fear.

My father and his father before him belonged to the Masons. They thought it was an innocent service organization. It is not a service organization. Those serving as leaders in the organization practice satanic rights and rituals. This is hidden to most who join and aptly called secret orders. When I found this out as a young adult, I repented for those generational sins, the open doors of my father and grandfather. I closed the doors they had opened to the enemy by the blood and authority of Jesus Christ. I did this so that moving forward, those sins would not be able to affect me, my children, or my grandchildren.

One time I counseled a woman who as a teenager had joined the International Order of Rainbow for Girls. Her step-grandparents were members of the Free Masons and Eastern Star. Rainbow Girls is an offshoot of those organizations. The grandparents encouraged her to join the organization under the pretense that she would be able to socialize better, and it would help her self-esteem.

As we were counseling, the Lord led me to ask her if she had ever made a vow. She looked surprised for a moment and then answered, "Yes, it was part of their initiation ceremony." During this ceremony, they blindfolded her and led her to different stations. At each one, she was required to make a verbal vow consisting of ritualistic memorized statements that caused her to align with something that was not of God. These oaths desensitized and bound her.

Secret Orders are but one example of what the Bible talks about in James 4:4: *You adulterous people, don't you know that friendship with the world is hatred toward God?* Participating in a secret order that demands unscriptural religious oaths and yokes you together with unbelievers is forbidden in God's Word (Matthew 5:33-37, 2 Cor. 6:14-7:1).

She didn't realize that the vows violated the first of the 10 Commandments:

You shall have no other gods before me (Exodus 20:3).

But above all, my brothers, do not swear either by heaven or by earth, or by any other oath, but let your "yes" be yes and your "no" be no, so that you may not fall under condemnation (James 5:12).

These vows had led to a myriad of problems for her in adulthood. She had spent a good deal of the 1980s involved in sex, drugs, and rock and roll as she was misdirected into thinking this was where she would find happiness. Many years later, she came to me for counseling. She repented to the Lord for making the vows, broke them in the name of Jesus, and closed the doors to the enemy associated with them. She also repented for joining that organization and closed other doors she had opened in her life. The open door of generational sins had caused her to continue to align with something that was not of God.

On another occasion, I counseled a young mother who, as a young girl, had attended a church that was actually a false religion. She remembered sitting in a circle with other girls that attended and making a vow. I had her renounce that vow and close the doors associated with it. Now she and her children are free to serve the Lord.

One day, while talking with Denise,[1] a grandmother, about some issues that were developing in her family, we started discussing fear. Fear is a root that leads to a stronghold that many people deal with in their lives, and it can also be connected generationally. I told her it felt like the problem was a generational stronghold of fear manifesting in her family as evidenced through the problems that were cropping up. Denise told me she did not feel like she herself struggled with this stronghold, but fear had a big grip on her grandmother's life.

As a child, she and her sister would spend time with their grandmother. Denise told me her grandmother had a way of speaking that would put fear on them. Fear had definitely taken root in Denise's sister's life. Denise had taken my class, Foundations of Faith, at church. I asked her if when we did the Open Door of Generational Sins, had she closed the generational stronghold of fear? She said she hadn't. She had thought because she did not personally struggle with fear, she did not need to close it. I explained she did because it was a generational stronghold in her family. She needed to close that open door over herself and her family, thus freeing the generations to come.

As a parent, you have the right to break the generational sins over your child. If you have already done so over the sins that came from your side of the family, it is also important to break those that were prevalent from your spouse's side of the family also.

Another important area to talk about is adoptions. It is so important for new adoptive parents and for those working as parents in the foster care system to break the generational strongholds and sins over their children. Generational open doors unfortunately can come along with these precious children. Most of the time we do not know what generational sins the parents and grandparents participated in. So, it is important to close open doors, generational strongholds, and sins in all four areas: Drugs and addiction, sexual immorality, the occult and false religion, and generational sins. It is critical that these parents have a special prayer time breaking these things off the child and dedicating them to the Lord.

In over 25 years of doing biblical counseling, I have seen many problems. It is so unfortunate how many of these problems stemmed from the open door of generational sins. The good news is that the Lord can redeem that. He can close those doors so that, moving forward, they will not affect you, your children, or grandchildren again.

But from everlasting to everlasting the Lord's love is with those who fear Him, and His righteousness with their children's children-with those who keep His covenant and remember to obey His precepts (Psalm 103:17-18).

The righteous who
walks in his integrity
Blessed are his
children after
him.

Proverbs 20:7

The following are some of the lies the enemy uses to get us to open a generational door ourselves and engage in that sin.

Lies of the Enemy Concerning Generational Sins

1. Well, if my parents, grandparents, aunts, uncles do it, it must be okay. - *Lie*

2. It's only a club, service organization, etc. They really only try to help people. - *Lie* (You need to find out and research what they stand for and what the leadership does in private.)

3. It's no big deal, it won't affect me or my kids. - *Lie*

4. All my family drinks. I need to do it to fit in and be socially accepted. - *Lie*

5. Vows—it's okay to make that vow. - *Lie* No, it's not! Pledging allegiance to something that is not of God breaks the commandment: You shall have no other gods before me.

6. Cults/False Religion/New Age: They are just trying to find God in their own way. - *Lie* (Rev. 22: 14-15)

7. Well, it didn't seem to hurt them. - *Lie* You don't know what that person has struggled with internally.

Scriptures to Help You Overcome in the Area of Generational Sins

Choose for yourselves this day whom you will serve, whether the gods which your fathers served that were on the other side of the river, or the gods of the Amorites, in whose land you dwell. But as for me and my house, we will serve the Lord (Joshua 24:15).

You shall not make for yourself a carved image, any likeness of anything that is in heaven above, or that is in the earth beneath, or that is in the water under the earth; you shall not bow down and serve them. For I, The Lord Your God, am a jealous God, visiting the iniquity of the fathers upon the children to the third and fourth generations of those who hate me, but showing mercy to thousands, to those who love me and keep my commandments (Exodus 20:4-6).

You shall have no other gods before me (Exodus 20:3).

The righteous who walks in his integrity-blessed are his children after him (Proverbs 20:7 ESV).

There are six things the Lord hates, seven that are an abomination to Him: haughty eyes, a lying tongue, hands that shed innocent blood, a heart that devises wicked plans, feet that make haste to run to evil, a false witness who breathes out lies, and one who sows discord among brothers (Proverbs 6:16-19 ESV).

The fear of the Lord is the beginning of wisdom (Proverbs 9:10).

For you did not receive a spirit that makes you a slave again to fear, but you received the spirit of sonship. And by Him we cry, "Abba, Father." The Spirit Himself testifies with our spirit that we are God's children (Romans 8:15-16).

But now thus says the Lord, he who created you, O Jacob, he who formed you, O Israel: Fear not, for I have redeemed you; I have called you by name, you are mine. When you pass through the waters, I will be with you; and through the rivers, they shall not overwhelm you; when you walk through fire you shall not be burned and the flame shall not consume you (Isaiah 43:1-2).

And do not get drunk with wine, for that is debauchery, but be filled with the Spirit, addressing one another in psalms and hymns and spiritual songs, singing and making melody to the Lord with your heart (Ephesians 5:18-19).

Wine is a mocker, strong drink a brawler, and whoever is led astray by it is not wise (Proverbs 20:1).

Who has woe? Who has sorrow? Who has strife? Who has complaints? Who has needless bruises? Who has bloodshot eyes? Those who linger over wine, those who go to sample mixed wine. Do not gaze at wine when it is red, when it sparkles in the cup, when it goes down smoothly. In the end it bites like a snake and poisons like a viper. Your eyes will see strange sights, and your mind will imagine confusing things. You will be like one sleeping on the high seas, lying on top of the rigging. "They hit me," you will say, "but I'm not hurt! They beat me, but I don't feel it! When will I wake up so I can find another drink?" (Proverbs 23:29-35)

Now the works of the flesh are evident: sexual immorality, impurity, sensuality, idolatry, sorcery, enmity, strife, jealousy, fits of anger, rivalries, dissensions, divisions, envy, drunkenness, orgies and things like these. I warn you, as I warned you before, that those who do such things will not inherit the Kingdom of God (Galatians 5:19-21).

---

[1] All names of clients have been changed throughout the book.
[2] Foundations of Faith is a class Caryn teaches at The Revival Center and is available on podcast at: Abba's Heart.com. Click the Resources tab, then click on Foundations of Faith

CREATE IN ME
a pure heart
O God,
AND RENEW A
Steadfast spirit
WITHIN ME

PSALM 51:10

⁓3⁓

THE OPEN DOOR OF SEXUAL IMMORALITY

Or do you not know that the unrighteous will not inherit the kingdom of God? Do not be deceived: neither the sexually immoral, nor idolaters, nor adulterers, nor men who practice homosexuality, nor thieves, nor the greedy, nor drunkards, nor revilers, nor swindlers will inherit the kingdom of God (1 Corinthians 6:9-10).

In today's society we have become overwhelmed with an epidemic of sexual immorality. Unfortunately, there is not much difference between Christians and the world in this area. Participating in sexual sin opens a door to the enemy. In the Bible, God has set boundaries for us through His Laws and Commandments for our protection. God condemns sexual immorality because He loves us and knows what is best for us.

Sexual Immorality: *Including but not limited to* Fornication, Adultery, Pornography, Promiscuity, Abortion, Abortion Pill, Morning After Pill, Molestation, Prostitution, Sex trafficking, Child Pornography, Internet Sex Sites, Phone Sex, Hook up Apps, Immoral Movies, Magazines, and Books, Bestiality, Masturbation, Rape, Incest, Lust, Sexual Fantasies, Orgies, Bi-Sexuality, Homosexuality, Lesbian, Trans-Sexual.

Sexual immorality can lead to many consequences such as sexually transmitted diseases, herpes, AIDS, abortion, infertility, broken marriages, and families, not to mention the regret, shame, and remorse it causes.

> *Flee from sexual immorality. All other sins a person commits are outside the body, but whoever sins sexually, sins against their own body* (1 Corinthians 6:18).

Believers are called in Christ to be morally and sexually pure. The word "pure" (Greek *hagnos* or *amiantos*) means to be free from all taint of that which is lewd. It means refraining from all acts and thoughts that incite desire not in accordance with one's virginity before marriage or one's marriage covenant after marriage. It stresses restraint and avoidance of all sexual activity that would defile one's purity before God.

The Bible teaches the following:

1. Sexual intimacy is reserved for the marriage relationship and is approved and blessed by God only in that state (Genesis 2:24, Song of Solomon 2:7, 4:12). Through marriage the husband and wife become one flesh.

> *Let marriage be held in honor among all; and let the marriage bed be undefiled, for God will judge the sexually immoral and adulterous* (Hebrews 13:4).

2. Adultery is expressly forbidden in scripture. Adultery is sex outside of the bonds of marriage, a breaking of the marriage covenant. (Exodus 20:14, Galatians 5: 19-21, Proverbs 6:32-33)

3. Fornication and sexual immorality before marriage is also expressly forbidden. It is listed in Galatians 5:19: *The acts of the sinful nature are obvious: sexual immorality, impurity and debauchery*. Sexual immorality (fornication) is any sexual activity or intercourse outside of the marriage union.

The book of Proverbs repeatedly warns about the destructiveness of sexual sins: Proverbs 2:16-19, 6:20-35, 22:14, 23:27-28, 29:3, 30:20, 31:3.

In Colossians 3:5, we are told to: *Put to death, therefore, whatever belongs to your earthly nature: sexual immorality, impurity, lust, evil desires.*

God condemns sexual immorality, but He offers deliverance.

Whether the immorality happened before or after marriage, Christ is the answer. Whether before or after salvation, Christ is the answer. The answer is true repentance, forgiveness, and turning away from that sin. Remember what Jesus told the woman caught in adultery after she had repented? He said, *"Go, and sin no more"* (John 8:1-11). It is far better to never open that door in the first place.

And that is what some of you were. But you were washed, you were sanctified, you were justified in the name of the Lord Jesus Christ and by the Spirit of our God (1 Corinthians 6:11).

As with all of our sins and open doors, God has dealt with immorality through the cross of Jesus Christ (1 Peter 2:24). There is hope. The Lord Jesus Christ loves you, and He has the tools to help you to overcome.

Keeping your mind and body pure is key in this area. More about this in chapter 8—Guarding Your Heart.

Many times, a sexual identity is formed through a molestation, though no fault of the child or young teen. The molestation can create gender identity issues leading them to believe they are homosexual because their first sexual experience was with someone of the same sex.

We must learn to exercise self-control in reference to all sexual matters before marriage and not open the door to sexual immorality. After marriage, sexual intimacy must be confined to one's marriage partner. The Bible names self-control as one aspect of the fruit of the spirit (Galatians 5:23). Our faithful commitment to

God and His Word with regard to purity in this area will result in our living as an overcomer, truly following the Lord.

Soul Ties

Through sexual immorality, soul ties are formed. When one has sex outside of the bonds of the marriage union, a soul tie is formed. The Bible says that when one marries, the two become one flesh. *Therefore, a man shall leave his father and mother and hold fast to his wife, and they shall become one flesh* (Genesis 2:24). The Bible states again in Ephesians 5:31 and Malachi 2:15 that *the two will become one flesh*. When a person has sex outside of the marriage union, a soul tie is formed.

> *Do you not know that he who unites himself with a prostitute is one with her in body? For it is said, the two will become one flesh* (1 Corinthians 6:16).

It is very important not to only close doors in this area of sexual immorality but to also break soul ties that were formed outside of the marriage union. All sexual unions that were participated in outside of marriage must be repented for and soul ties broken.

You can close the door to sexual immorality, but failure to break the soul tie to the other person can result in your still having feelings or being drawn to that person. A connection with them will linger.

An example of the prayer to break soul ties:

Dear Lord, please forgive me for having sex with: _____, _____, and _____. (List the names of person(s) you have had sex with outside of marriage.) I repent and ask you to forgive me and I break the soul ties formed with _____, _____, and _____. In the name of Jesus Christ, I pray.

Sex can also be a demonic highway. Someone with demonic bondages can pass them spiritually to another person through sexual intercourse. I have counseled people that this has happened to.

The open doorway of sexual immorality often can lead from one immoral behavior to another in an increasing need to satisfy the flesh. When counseling, I have noted that when a young woman does not get the male attention she needs from her father, she will often turn to young men in sexual ways to meet that psychological need.

In the area of abortion, many women I have counseled have dealt with extreme grief and remorse. Many of them have suffered silently for years.

Take Linda[3] for example. Linda was in her late fifties when she came to me for counseling. She was a believer and as we went through the first session of biblical counseling, we talked about her earliest childhood memories (ECM), her parents and family, and her grief over her son being murdered at a young age. She seemed to be giving me all the right answers. She had mourned her son, but this wasn't the area where she was stuck in, so to speak.

At the end of the first session I said to her, "There seems to be a disconnect, Linda. You came to me for counseling, but yet you are saying you are fine in all the areas we have talked about. Is there something you are not telling me?"

She hesitated, then broke down sobbing and admitted a secret she had held for many years. She told me that when she was a teenager, she had become pregnant with her boyfriend's baby. She wanted to have the baby, but her mother was distraught. Her older sisters had already become pregnant out of wedlock, and she (Linda) was her mother's last chance to have one daughter not having a child out of wedlock. Her mother did not listen to Linda when she said she wanted to have the baby but instead marched her down to the clinic to perform an abortion.

Linda tried to bury this secret for many years. Finally, during counseling, it came out. Years of regret, grief, and remorse (for not standing up to her mother), and shame came pouring out as we prayed and closed that door. As she asked the Lord to forgive her, He beautifully set her free that day. She became free from the weight of that sin and secret, free to become who Jesus had made her to be, and free to walk in her calling. The enemy had used this open door in her life to hold her back from walking in freedom in her calling. I assured her, "It is never too late. The Lord still has a work for you to do!"

Another time when I was counseling another woman in the area of open doors, she told me she had confessed her sin of abortion to the Lord and had asked Him to forgive her literally hundreds of times but never felt set free. As we prayed and closed her open doors in the area of sexual immorality, the Lord showed me that although she had told the Lord she was sorry and had repented for the abortion many times, she had never allowed Him to cleanse her. First John 1:9 says: *If we confess our sins, He is faithful and just to forgive us our sins and to cleanse us from all unrighteousness.* As I told her what the Lord had shown me, she started sobbing. She asked the Lord to come and cleanse her from all unrighteousness, the sin of abortion, and closed the door to sexual immorality. She was truly set free that day.

The second part of 1 John 1:9 is true in every area of open door sins. As we confess our sins and ask Him to forgive us of them, we must allow Him to cleanse us from all unrighteousness. Cleansing is such an important part of confession and repentance.

Many men and women open the door to sexual immorality as teens. Once that door is open, many are plagued with immoral thoughts and/or behaviors. This happens because they do not know how to break soul ties and close doors they have opened to sexual immorality. They have never learned how to take captive every thought (2 Cor. 10:4-5), or how to sanctify their minds with the reading of the Word of God, the Bible.

This is especially true of the open door of pornography. Once considered a "man's" sinful habit, I have seen many women participating in this open door sin, a trap of the enemy. With the increasing availability of internet porn (readily available on phones and computers), hook up apps, and apps that promote sending of sexual pictures, many young women are finding themselves addicted as well.

Today, men and women are constantly bombarded with sexually immoral television shows, commercials, movies, songs, music, videos, billboards, books, magazines, computer sites, and ads. Once you click on something immoral, more and more sites will have your address. With pornography so easily accessible, many open this door and fall into the trap of the enemy. Just as the open door of drugs stalls your emotional development, pornography can do the same as well.

But there is a choice. Say NO to the open door of sexual immorality. Close that door and do not re-open it! Exercise self-control and keep your mind and body pure, focusing on the things of God and not the world.

Overcoming Temptation

Once the open door of sexual immorality is closed, the following are some steps to take to overcome temptation and to keep the door to sexual immorality closed:

1. Take captive every thought and make it obedient to Christ, purpose in your heart and mind to resist temptation and keep the door to sexual immorality closed (2 Cor. 10:4-5, Matthew 6:13, Hebrews 2:18, 1 Cor. 10:13).

2. Renew and sanctify your mind through the reading of the Word of God, the Bible (Romans 12:1-2, see chapter 10-Renewing Your Mind).

3. Guard your heart from everything that defiles (Proverbs 4:23, see chapter 8: Guarding Your Heart).

4. Avoid every person or place of compromise (1 Cor. 15:33; Psalm 101).

5. Clean your home, computer, and phone out of everything that is immoral (Psalm 51:10, see chapter 12: Walking it Out—Keeping your Spiritual and Physical House Clean).

Remember, the Word of God, either preached or written cannot effectively take hold in our lives if we are not separated from moral filth, immoral behavior, and evil actions.

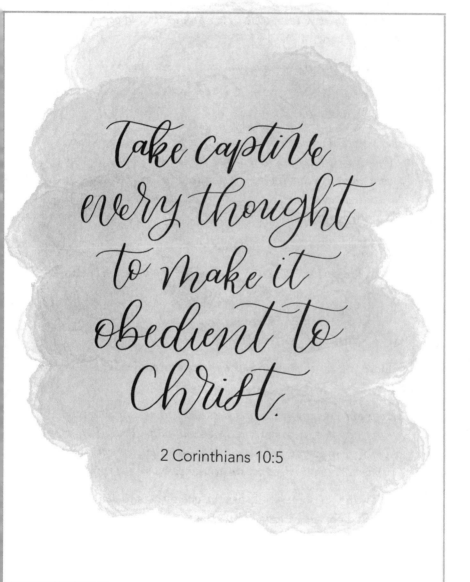

Take captive every thought to make it obedient to Christ.

2 Corinthians 10:5

Use Scripture to Overcome Sexual Immorality

Submit yourselves then to God. Resist the devil, and he will flee from you (James 4:7).

Take captive every thought and make it obedient to Christ (2 Corinthians 10:5).

Resist temptation.

No temptation has seized you except what is common to man. And God is faithful; He will not let you be tempted beyond what you can bear. But when you are tempted, He will also provide a way out so that you can stand up under it (1 Corinthians 10:13).

Train yourself to be godly (1 Timothy 4:7).

Feed your spiritual man and not your sinful nature (Galatians 6:7-8).

Pray Psalm 51:10: *Create in me a pure heart O God, and renew a steadfast spirit within me.*

The more you do these things the easier it becomes. The choice is yours.

How can a young man (or woman) keep his way pure? By living according to your Word. I seek you with all my heart; do not let me stray from your commands. I have hidden your Word in my heart that I might not sin against you (Psalm 119:9-11).

The following are some of the lies the enemy uses to get us to open the door and engage in sexual immorality.

Lies of the Enemy Concerning Sexual Immorality

1. It's okay because we really love each other. - *Lie* Sex before marriage is self-seeking. It appears to be love but is really lust.

2. If you're in a committed relationship, it's okay. - *Lie*

3. It's okay because we are going to get married in the future. - *Lie*

4. Just this once. - *Lie*

5. If you really love me, you will have sex with me. - *Lie*

6. If you really love me, you will show me. - *Lie*

7. I really need this physical release. - *Lie*

8. Pornography—I will just look at this one time. - *Lie* It hooks you and leads you down a very bad path.

9. It's okay to watch this porn movie or look at the website. It won't affect me. -*Lie* Now you've contaminated your mind with bad visuals.

10. I will stop doing porn once I get married. - *Lie* Porn is very addictive, and you will always compare your spouse with the visuals you have seen, and she/he will never be enough or be able to compare or compete with that.

11. These are lies of the enemy in the area of adultery: My spouse isn't paying enough attention to me - *Lie* Why are you so needy? Go to Jesus to meet your needs.

12. My spouse doesn't understand me. - *Lie* Jesus understands you. Go to Him.

13. This other person makes me feel loved, happy, wanted, etc. - *Lie* Go to the Lord for your needs.

14. The grass looks greener on the other side. –*Lie* Do not even look. Jesus said that anyone who even looks at a woman lustfully has already committed adultery with her in his heart (Matthew 5:28).

Scriptures to Help you Fight Sexual Immorality

Put to death, therefore, whatever belongs to your earthly nature: sexual immorality, impurity, lust, evil desires (Colossians 3:5).

For the mind set on the flesh is death, but the mind set on the Spirit is life and peace (Romans 8:6 NASB).

The night is nearly over; the day is almost here. So, let us put aside the deeds of darkness and put on the armor of light. Let us behave decently, as in the daytime, not in orgies and drunkenness, not in sexual immorality and debauchery, not in dissension and jealousy. Rather clothe yourselves with the Lord Jesus Christ, and do not think about how to gratify the desires of the sinful nature (Romans 13:12-14).

The acts of the sinful nature are obvious: sexual immorality, impurity and debauchery; idolatry and witchcraft; hatred, discord, jealousy, fits of rage, selfish ambition, dissensions, factions and envy; drunkenness orgies, and the like. I warn you, as I did before, that those who live like this will not inherit the kingdom of God (Galatians 5:19-21).

Therefore do not let sin reign in your mortal body so that you obey its lusts, and do not go on presenting the members of your body to sin as instruments of unrighteousness; but present yourselves to God as those alive from the dead, and your members as instruments of righteousness to God. For sin shall not be master over you, for you are not under law but under grace (Romans 6:12-14 NASB).

Turn my heart toward your statutes and not toward selfish gain. Turn my eyes away from worthless things; preserve my life according to your Word (Psalm 119:36-37).

The Open Door of Sexual Immorality

But among you there must not be even a hint of sexual immorality, or of any kind of impurity, or of greed, because these are improper for God's holy people. Nor should there be obscenity, foolish talk or coarse joking, which are out of place, but rather thanksgiving. For of this you can be sure: No immoral, impure or greedy person–such a man is an idolater–has any inheritance in the kingdom of Christ and of God (Ephesians 5:3-5).

Do you not know that the wicked will not inherit the kingdom of God? Do not be deceived. Neither the sexually immoral nor idolater nor adulterers nor male prostitutes nor homosexual offenders nor thieves nor the greedy nor drunkards nor slanders nor swindlers will inherit the kingdom of God. And that is what some of you were. But you were washed, you were sanctified, you were justified and the name of the Lord Jesus Christ and by the Spirit of our God (1 Corinthians 6:9-11).

Food is for the stomach and the stomach for food–but God will destroy them both. The body is not meant for sexual immorality, but for the Lord, and the Lord for the body (1 Corinthians 6:13).

For the flesh sets its desire against the Spirit, and the Spirit against the flesh; for these are in opposition to one another, so that you may not do the things that you please (Galatians 5:17 NASB).

Make every effort to live in peace with everyone and to be holy; without holiness no one will see the Lord (Hebrews 12:14).

For it is written: "Be holy because I am holy" (1 Peter 1:16).

Blessed are the pure in heart, for they shall see God (Matthew 5:8).

Flee from sexual immorality. All other sins a person commits are outside the body, but whoever sins sexually, sins against their own body (1 Corinthians 6:18).

Marriage should be honored by all, and the marriage bed kept pure, for God will judge the adulterer and all the sexually immoral (Hebrews 13:4).

You shall not commit adultery (Exodus 20:14).

Jesus replied: Do not murder, do not commit adultery, do not steal, do not give false testimony (Matthew 19:18).

The one who commits adultery with a woman is lacking sense; He who would destroy himself does it. Wounds and disgrace he will find, and his reproach will not be blotted out (Proverbs 6:32-33 NASB).

No temptation has seized you except what is common to man. And God is faithful; He will not let you be tempted beyond what you can bear. But when you are tempted, He will provide a way out so that you can stand up under it (1 Corinthians 10:13).

Above all else, guard your heart for it is the wellspring of life (Proverbs 4:23).

Jesus said: What comes out of a man is what makes him unclean. For from within, out of men's hearts, come evil thoughts, sexual immorality, theft, murder, adultery, greed, malice, deceit, lewdness, envy, slander, arrogance and folly. All these evils come from inside and make a man unclean (Mark 7:20-23).

Submit yourselves, then to God. Resist the devil, and he will flee from you (James 4:7).

Therefore God gave them over in the sinful desires of their hearts to sexual impurity for the degrading of their bodies with one another. They exchanged the truth of God for a lie, and worshiped and served created things rather that the Creator-who is forever praised. Amen (Rom. 1:24-32).

For if you live according to the flesh you will die; but if by the Spirit you put to death the deeds of the body, you will live (Rom. 8:13).

Blessed are those who wash their robes, that they may have the right to the tree of life and may go through the gates into the city. Outside are the dogs, those who practice magic arts, the sexually immoral, the murderers, the idolaters and everyone who loves and practices falsehood (Rev. 22: 14-15).

For God alone has become my Savior. He alone is my safe place.

～4～

THE OPEN DOOR OF DRUGS AND ADDICTION

In the same way, count yourselves dead to sin, but alive to God in Christ Jesus. Therefore, do not let sin reign in your mortal body so that you obey its evil desires. Do not offer any part of yourself to sin as an instrument of wickedness (Romans 6:11-13).

A drug is any substance that produces a physical, mental, or psychological change in the user, such as alcohol, drugs, or anything that alters your brain or your body.

I am including addiction in this chapter because addiction will cause a door to the enemy to be opened through alcohol, drug, and substance abuse, along with gambling and gaming addictions, sexual addictions (see chapter 3), and eating addictions. Addictions cause you to come into bondage to that sin. They are called life-dominating sins. A life-dominating sin is one that takes control over your life. It is something that you habitually do.

Drugs: *Including, but not limited to* Alcohol (Alcoholism), Marijuana, (Cannabis), Meth, Crank, (methamphetamine), Barbiturates, LSD (Lysergic Acid Diethylamide), Heroin, Hashish, Opium, Buttons-Mescaline, Cocaine, PCP, Angel Dust, Hallucinogenic Mushrooms-Psilocybin, Anabolic Steroids, gym candy, Crack, Speed, Uppers, Amphetamines,

Black Beauties, Hearts, Sedatives, Vaping, Inhaling/Huffing, (Inhalants), Fentanyl, GHB, MDMA, Ecstasy, Ketamine, Buprenorphine, Methadone, Morphine, Benzodiazepines, Phencyclidine, Stimulants, Depressants, Opioids, Oxycodone, (Opiates), misuse of prescription drugs.

Addictions: *Including but not limited to* Alcoholism, Drug Addiction, Substance Abuse, Pornography, Sexual Addictions, Eating Addictions, Anorexia, Bulimia, Video Gaming, Gambling, etc.

Even if you have only used drugs "one time," that one time opened a door to the enemy that must be closed. Closing this door will give you the freedom in Christ to finally put this lifestyle and sin behind you. You will be free to walk with the Lord as an overcomer.

A lot of people who do drugs and abuse alcohol do so in an effort to escape reality. The drug and addiction doors are ones that, if not closed, the person will continually be drawn back into a cycle of that sin controlling their lives.

Whenever you continually practice a particular sin, you place yourself under its control. While enslaved by that sin, you cannot legitimately claim to be wholeheartedly following Jesus Christ. If you persistently continue to practice this sin and do not take biblical steps to overcome it, you have reason to doubt the genuineness of your salvation. In spite of your own inherent inability to overcome the bondage of a life-dominating sin, God's grace, mercy, and power have been provided for you as a sincere believer in Jesus Christ *to overcome any sin*. Furthermore, as you overcome sin's power by God's enablement, the character of Christ is developed in your life.

Scriptures: Romans 6:1-14, 22, 8:2; Psalm 119:9-11; Ephesians 2:1-10; 5:18-20; 6:10-13; 2 Timothy 2:22; Hebrews 10:26-27; 2 Peter 1:2-10; 1 John 1:6-2:6; 3:4-10; 4:4; 5:5.[4]

Characteristics of a Life-Dominating Sin or Addiction

1. You practice this sin even though you have tried repeatedly to stop.

2. You practice this sin and blame others or circumstances for your failure to stop.

3. You deny that what you are doing is sin.

4. You convince yourself that you are not enslaved to this sin and can stop at any time, even though you continue to do this sin.

5. You repeat the sin even though any pleasure or satisfaction to yourself is short-lived while the harm to yourself and others is considerable and long term.

6. You seek to hide your sin and lie on a regular basis.

7. You still commit this sin although you know that it obscures the testimony of Jesus Christ in your life and is a stumbling block to others.

8. You still continue in this sin despite the knowledge that God's Word tells you to stop sinning and that God's provisions are sufficient to release you from this bondage.

9. You repeatedly commit this sin while knowing that this does not please the Lord nor bring glory to God.

10. You continue in this sin even though you realize that your deeds (thoughts, words, and actions) do not conform to the character of Christ.[2]

There are two types of addiction

1. Chemical—this refers to addiction that involves the use of substances.

2. Behavioral—this refers to addiction that involves compulsive

behaviors. These are persistent, repeated behaviors that you carry out even if they don't offer any real benefit.

As addiction develops, it is common to lose interest in hobbies, activities, and other things you once enjoyed. Many of the roots of drug and alcohol dependency, as well as many other addictions, are founded in: insecurity, low self-worth, a poor self-image, guilt, fear, and rebellion.

When there is a lack of identity in a person's life, they are more prone to develop an addiction, including embracing a false identity such as when you embrace the sinful nature (please read Galatians 5:13-21, 6:7-8) and exalt anything (idolatry) above Jesus Christ. The source of all addiction and behavioral issues comes from exalting self and embracing a false identity. Knowing who you are in Jesus Christ (identity) overcomes this.

When there is a spiritual void, an absence of God, in the user's life, they will be especially vulnerable to drug abuse, alcohol abuse, substance abuse, and addictive behaviors as they are looking for something to fill that void.

Drugs and alcohol can also be introduced generationally through a parent or a sibling who is a drug user or alcohol abuser and involved, modeled, and/or encouraged use at a young age.

Drug use is especially detrimental to a young user due to the neurological pathways in the brain that are not yet fully developed. This area is on the prefrontal cortex and is where decision making is formed. It affects thinking, planning, problem solving, sensory processing, and decision making.

Another thing that drugs will do, besides destroy your life and the lives of those around you, is stall your emotional development. When counseling drug users, I have found that their emotional development was stalled at very close to the age when they first started using the drugs. This also can be true of those who form sexual addictions, such as pornography. Through counseling, we help the person to progress to age appropriate behavior.

Many times, a person's ability to be honest determines their ability to recover and thus be well.

Drug dependency and addiction affect the whole person: spiritual, physical, mental, emotional, and social. Drug use and alcohol abuse trap the user in a cycle of intoxication, bingeing, withdrawal, and craving.

Take Candice, for example. When I met her, she was a drug addicted mother of three. She shared with me that her many years of drug abuse had started at the young age of twelve. Her parents had tried to the best of their ability to raise her and her siblings. They took her to church. She remembered them reading the Bible to her as a child. On the surface, things looked good. Where was the disconnect? Why did the drug use start at age twelve? As we delved into her childhood during counseling, I discovered she had been sexually molested as a young child, at four years of age.

A family "friend," in reality a pedophile, had molested her under the guise of babysitting for the family. She did not tell her parents of this horror. I think the reason she didn't tell them was because she did not feel safe. Her mother was constantly disapproving of her, being mean and verbally abusive to Candice, who had a tender heart. While her father was loving and kind towards Candice, he never stopped her mother's mistreatment of her.

Since she did not feel safe with her parents, she turned to a life of drugs. She used them to cope with her feelings of shame and guilt. She felt dirty. She had overwhelming feelings of wanting to punish herself. All of this stemmed from the molestation. She was hoping the drugs would make her problems go away. She wanted to escape. We know this only exasperated her problems.

She started using marijuana at twelve and then came pills: black beauties, pink hearts, and cross tops. Soon these didn't satisfy, and she progressed to using cocaine by fifteen years of age. She used the drugs to escape reality and how she felt about herself. Thus began her cycle of drug use and running away.

Usually after about a month of being gone, she would call her parents to come pick her up and take her home, only to leave again, over and over for the drugs. Several times her parents put her into in-house treatment centers for drug dependency. She told me the counselors there would say to her: "Don't use, don't use, don't use!" But they never gave her the tools of how not to use or get to the root of her problems. She would even run away from these programs, not an easy feat I'm sure!

Her constant drug use continued well into her forties. By then she had progressed to smoking meth and snorting crank every day. One day, she wandered into our church. She remembers thinking that Jesus was exactly what she needed. She was dying physically and spiritually from her life of drugs.

When she walked into church for the first time, she laid her eyes upon a life-sized version of the Cross that Jesus had died upon. Complete with the crown of thorns and splatters of blood. She thought: *That is the most beautiful thing I've ever seen.* She realized she had been selfish, living for herself and forgetting what Jesus had done for her. She saw that her sins had crucified Jesus on the Cross. The shame, guilt, and pain of her life of drug abuse and running overwhelmed her. She fell to her knees and repented. She told the Lord she was sorry and asked Him to forgive her.

Her salvation was the beginning of a long road of recovery. Candice needed to close all of the open doors in her life, learn how to overcome the drugs, and walk with the Lord.

Our pastor asked me to call her and start counseling. She was high the first time I called. She started the process of biblical counseling: closing doors, reading the Bible, memorizing scripture, doing Bible homework, attending the Foundations of Faith class,[3] being accountable to me and not lying, working on her emotional development, and faithful church attendance.

We were able to get to roots of her problem: unworthiness, addiction, fear, and insecurity with root symptoms of shame, anger, guilt, and low self-worth, stemming from the molestation. These roots had led to her drug use.

Candice stated to me that learning this key of how to close the open door of drugs in her life has been life changing. Jesus is Lord of her life now, not the drugs.

So if the Son sets you free, you are truly free (John 8:36 NLT). Jesus wants for you to be free too!

Invaluable Principles to Overcome Drugs and Addictions

1. The Word of God, the Bible. Reading and especially memorizing scriptures. Scripture memorization brings healing to your mind.

2. Prayer. Develop a lifestyle of prayer. Also, it is very important for you to tell the enemy to leave you alone. For you to verbalize this out loud. James 4:7-10.

3. You must completely sever the friendships you have made with other drug users, pushers, and others with addictions. Forming new friendships with those that are mature in the faith.

4. Resolving the root of the problem. (See chapter 7.) Discovering what led to the drug, addiction, or substance abuse in the first place.

5. You need to develop an outward focus. Your focus has been inward, focused on yourself, your needs, your next fix. Remember, Jesus always had an outward focus. So should you!

6. You must purpose in your heart to please the Lord, preferring Him, and not gratifying the desires of the sinful nature (Galatians 6:7-8).

7. Find someone to walk with you through this journey of recovery, an accountability partner or friend, one who is mature in the Lord.

The following are some of the lies the enemy uses to get us to open the door and engage in drug use and addictive behavior.

Lies of the Enemy Concerning Drugs and Addiction

1. I will just smoke pot this one time. - *Lie* It opens a door to the enemy.

2. I won't be cool; I won't fit in or be socially accepted if I don't do it. - *Lie*

3. Everyone is doing it. - *Lie*

4. It won't lead to other drugs. - *Lie* Marijuana is a gateway drug. It opens a door to the enemy. You will continually need more drugs and or alcohol to achieve that high.

5. To rebel against authority or parents. - *Lie* You are rebelling against God.

6. The drugs/alcohol will help me to feel better. - *Lie*

7. Oh, it's not that bad. - *Lie* This is a lie the enemy uses in many sins.

8. I just want to escape and forget about my problems. This is probably the biggest lie. Every drug addict I have counseled has used this lie of the enemy to excuse why they have used drugs. So I ask them: "Did your problems go away or disappear as a result of your using drugs? What happened when you came down from your drug induced high?" "No, they reply, "the problems were still there, and they got even worse."

9. I can hold my liquor. I won't get drunk. - *Lie*

10. It helps me to relax. - *Lie* You do not need alcohol or drugs to relax.

11. I will just do it one more time. - *Lie* You need to admit you are trapped in a cycle of addictive behavior.

Scriptures to Help you to Overcome Drugs and Addiction

May the God of hope fill you with all joy and peace as you trust in Him, so that you may overflow with hope by the power of the Holy Spirit (Romans 15:13).

I can do all things through Him who gives me strength (Philippian 4:13).

But each person is tempted when they are dragged away by their own evil desire and enticed. Then after desire is conceived, it gives birth to sin, and sin, when it is full grown, gives birth to death (James 1:14-15).

No temptation has seized you except what is common to man. And God is faithful; He will not let you be tempted beyond what you can bear. But when you are tempted, He will also provide a way out so that you can stand up under it (1 Corinthians 10:13).

He who conceals his sins does not prosper, but whoever confesses and renounces them finds mercy (Proverbs 28:13).

If we say we have no sin, we deceive ourselves, and the truth is not in us. If we confess our sins, He is faithful and just to forgive us our sins and to cleanse us from all unrighteousness (1 John 1:8-9).

For you have spent enough time in the past doing what pagans choose to do—living in debauchery, lust, drunkenness, orgies, carousing and detestable idolatry (1 Peter 4:3).

Turn my heart toward your statutes and not toward selfish gain. Turn my eyes away from worthless things; preserve my life according to your Word (Psalm 119:36-37).

Only be careful that this liberty of yours, this power to choose, does not somehow become a stumbling block, that is a temptation to sin, to the weak (1 Corinthians 8:9 AMP).

But understand this, that in the last days there will come times of difficulty. For people will be lovers of self, lovers of money, proud, arrogant, abusive, disobedient to their parents, ungrateful, unholy, heartless, unappeasable, slanderous, without self-control, brutal, not loving good, treacherous, reckless, swollen with conceit, lovers of pleasure rather than lovers of God, having the appearance of godliness but denying its power. Avoid such people (2 Timothy 3:1-5).

So if the Son sets you free, you will be free indeed (John 8:36).

The thief comes only to steal and kill and destroy. I came that they may have life and have it abundantly (John 10:10).

Wine is a mocker and beer a brawler; whoever is led astray by them is not wise (Proverbs 20:1).

Do not be drunk on wine, which leads to debauchery. Instead be filled with the Spirit (Ephesians 5:18).

Who has woe? Who has sorrow? Who has strife? Who has complaints? Who has needless bruises? Who has bloodshot eyes? Those who linger over wine, who go to sample bowls of mixed wine. Do not gaze at wine when it is red, when it sparkles in the cup, when it goes down smoothly! In the end it bites like a snake and poisons like a viper. Your eyes will see strange sights and your mind imagine confusing things. You will be like one sleeping on the high seas, lying on top of the rigging. "They hit me", you will say, "but I'm not hurt!" "They beat me, but I don't feel it! When will I wake up so I can find another drink?" (Proverbs 23:29-35)

You will keep him in perfect peace, whose mind is stayed on You, because he trusts in You (Isaiah 26:3).

For God has not given us a spirit of fear, but of power and of love and a sound mind (2 Timothy 1:7).

Therefore, if anyone is in Christ, he is a new creation; the old has gone, the new has come! (2 Corinthians 5:17)

In the same way, count yourselves dead to sin but alive to God in Christ Jesus. Therefore, do not let sin reign in your mortal body so that you obey its evil desires. Do not offer the parts of your body to sin, as instruments of wickedness, but rather offer yourselves to God, as those who have been brought from death to life; and offer the parts of your body to him as instruments of righteousness (Romans 6:11-13).

---

[1] Referenced from *Biblical Counseling Foundation: Self-Confrontation, A Manual for In-Depth Biblical Discipleship.*

[2] *Referenced from Biblical Counseling Foundation: Self-Confrontation, A Manual for In-Depth Biblical Discipleship.*

[3] *Foundations of Faith is a class Caryn teaches at The Revival Center and is available on podcast at: Abba's Heart.com. Click the Resources tab, then click on Foundations of Faith*

FOR I KNOW THE
plans
I HAVE FOR YOU
declares the Lord,
PLANS TO
prosper you
AND NOT TO HARM YOU
plans to give
YOU
hope and A
future.

JEREMIAH 29:11

~5~

THE OPEN DOOR OF THE OCCULT AND FALSE RELIGION

"When you participate in any occult activity, you are playing with the devil's weapons." —*Rev. Sandra Querin*

The meaning of the word "occult" from Webster's dictionary is: To conceal, hidden, secret, mysterious, of mystic arts, such as magic, astrology, etc. Involvement in the occult opens the door to spiritual bondage and to the enemy.

Many people today are seeking power. Unfortunately, some do not seek God, through Jesus Christ, the true source of life and power. They are blinded by the god of this age, the devil (2 Corinthians 4:4) and seek a power that is not of God. They do not understand that the Bible strictly warns and forbids people about involvement in such activities:

Let no one be found among you who sacrifices his son or daughter in the fire, who practices divination or sorcery, interprets omens, engages in witchcraft, or casts spells, or who is a medium or spiritist or who consults the dead. Anyone who does these things is detestable to the Lord, and because of these detestable practices the Lord your God will drive out those nations before you (Deuteronomy 18:10-12).

The Spirit clearly says that in later times some will abandon the faith and follow deceiving spirits and things taught by demons (1 Timothy 4:1).

The main way a Christian can (or will) be deceived is by not having knowledge of what the Word of God says through not reading the Bible enough and not hiding the Word in their heart (Psalm 119:11).

There are so many things in today's world that desensitize people to the dangers of the occult: occult movies and books, television, games, horoscopes, video games, occult toys and even occult influenced cartoons.

The Occult/False Religion: *Including, but not limited to* witchcraft, sorcery, black magic, white magic, wicca, psychics, spells, voodoo, tarot cards, horoscopes, astrology, fortune telling, palm readers, tea leaf readings, spiritism, cleansings, seances, horror movies, dungeons and dragons, Ouija board, Magic the Gathering, Harry Potter books and movies, Twilight movies and books, occult movies, books, and video games, Halloween, Pokémon, crystals, reiki, chakra, acupuncture, reincarnation, channeling, telepathy, hypnosis, worship of demons, magic arts, occult toys and cartoons, astral projection, clairvoyance, extrasensory perception, Eastern religions, cults, false religion, New Age, transcendental meditation, yoga (most), visualization, the law of attraction.

Remember this: Anyone or anything that has a power that is not from God is from the enemy.

There are so many occult, new age philosophies, false religion ideas, and theories out there, which is why I have listed in the section above "Including but not limited to." If you feel a check in your spirit, or if it does not line up and agree with the Bible, don't do it! Listen to the Holy Spirit.

Dear friends, do not believe every spirit, but test the spirits to see whether they are from God, because many false prophets have gone out into the world. This is how you can recognize the Spirit of God; Every spirit that acknowledges that Jesus Christ has come in the flesh is from God, but every spirit that does not acknowledge Jesus is not from God. This is the spirit of the antichrist, which you have heard is coming and even now is already in the world (1 John 4:1-3).

The New Age Movement

The New Age Movement is a spiritual, political and social network brought together through common interests in occult and pagan beliefs. Eastern religions are especially favored by those involved in new age, all religions are accepted as equal except for Christianity, which teaches there is only one way to God, through Jesus Christ. To the New Age follower, their god is merely an impersonal consciousness or force that is part of the earth and universe. They see themselves as part of god. Or even think that they are all gods. They seek altered states of consciousness through meditation, hypnosis, visualization, the law of attraction, clairvoyance, channeling, telepathy, astral projection, and many times drugs.[1]

The New Age Movement is the latest of mankind's age-old desire to be a god while rejecting Jesus Christ and the one true God. See Genesis 3:4-5.

For the time will come when men will not put up with sound doctrine. Instead to suit their own desires, they will gather around them a great number of teachers to say what their itching ears want to hear. They will turn their ears away from the truth and turn aside to myths (2 Timothy 4:3-4).

Cults and False Religion

A cult or a false religion can be defined as a religious group that teaches doctrines and beliefs that deviate from Christian doctrine and what the Bible teaches. This includes New Age religions and new thought philosophies. They are a false work. (I am not talking here about a mainstream branch of Christianity that differs doctrinally from what you believe.)

Cults and false religion either distort the truth or focus on half-truths. The small amount of truth that they do proclaim is often mixed with doctrinal error and is, therefore, very dangerous. It is so important to always let the Bible interpret the Bible. Always use the scriptures before and after a passage to interpret a particular scripture. Take the chapters before and after in context also.

Cults and false religion many times teach salvation by works and not by grace. This opposes Ephesians 2:8-9: *For it is by grace you have been saved, through faith—and this not from yourselves, it is the gift of God—not by works, so that no one boast.* The Gospel is a free gift of God. Period. We do not earn it.

Cults and false religion thrive on ignorance and uncertainty. Christians who do not know what they believe or what the Bible says are especially vulnerable. Deception is one of the enemy's key tools. The less we read the Bible, the weaker we become and the more prone we are to compromise, making us more susceptible to the enemy's deception and his schemes.

Cults and false religion also teach extra-biblical or special revelations. They add to or take away from the Bible, opposing Revelation 22:18-19 (NLT):

And I solemnly declare to everyone who hears the words of prophecy written in this book: If anyone adds anything to what is written here, God will add to that person the plagues described in this book. And if anyone removes any of the words from this book of prophecy, God will remove that person's share in the tree of life and in the holy city that are described in this book.

And of course, cults and false religion either deny Jesus Christ as the one and only true Son of God who died on the Cross for our sins, or they relegate Him to a place that is lesser than the Son of God. Cults and false religion often renounce the deity of Christ, declaring they themselves are equal to Jesus Christ. In so doing, they minimize the cross.

Many Christian churches are lax in their responsibility to teach God's Word. They fail to proclaim the whole truth of God's Word for fear of offense or a desire to be "politically correct." Many times, churches also fail to teach and disciple new believers. They become program driven, in an effort to be "seeker friendly."

The enemy is good at what he does. He markets himself to children at an early age. There is a generation of children that are being desensitized to the dangers of the occult. Occult toys, games, books, cartoons, comic books, and video games are aimed at getting children to have an affinity towards evil and the occult. When it is time for the child to choose Jesus as Lord, he or she is already drawn toward the "dark side," having been desensitized.

The books and movies of Harry Potter are but one example of this. It has been said that these books and movies have been the largest recruiting tool for the occult in decades. Children, curious after reading in the books about the spells and occult activities portrayed in them, do a search on the internet to find out more about this "power" and are drawn into the world of the occult.

The Harry Potter books focus on the plight of young Harry, who is selected to attend the prestigious thousand-year-old Hogwarts School of Witchcraft and Wizardry. Harry is an orphan. His parents, who were practitioners of "white magic," were murdered by the evil Lord Voldemort, a master of the "dark arts." When Lord Voldemort, the most powerful dark wizard for a century put the curse that had killed so many witches and wizards onto Harry Potter, it rebounded upon Voldemort, ripping him from his body.

Some other things to note from the books: Harry's blood is given magical powers. Harry is taught at Hogwarts how to use magic tools, spells, rituals, and curses. According to Rev. Robert Frisken of Christian Community Schools in Australia, "The ordinary person in these books is typified as being bad because they have no magic powers. And the heroes are the people who are using the occult."[2] Harry Potter is witchcraft repackaged to be appealing to children. It promotes an interest in magic and the occult and is so dangerous.

Witchcraft Is Not Fantasy but a Sinful Reality in Our World

The acts of the sinful nature are obvious: sexual immorality, impurity and debauchery; idolatry and witchcraft (Galatians 5:19-20).

The Pokémon Go app is an occult rooted and demon-oriented game of witchcraft. Players, many times children, chase and empower virtual demons. *Pokémon* is a Japanese word that means "pocket monster." It is a game that comes from the same company that originally developed "Dungeons and Dragons" and "Magic the Gathering" games. These are highly occultic and anti-Christian games.

Discernment is a spiritual gift of the Holy Spirit (1 Corinthians 12:1-11). I believe that this is a gift we all need in today's world. Adults and children need the ability to discern between what is of God and what isn't (1 John 4:1-3). Ask the Lord to increase your discernment and teach your children how to discern between good and evil.

Video Games

Some people think they are innocently playing video games. Many times, these games are occult influenced, or they contain excessive violence, sexual immorality, and ungodly actions. The compulsion to play them is so strong and addictive that people play them for hours on end. The games draw the player into a world of fantasy and make believe. Video games, which put the player into a false or virtual reality intending to alter your soul, need to be avoided.

He who works his land will have abundant food, but he who chases fantasies lacks judgement (Proverbs 12:11).

Many times video games distract a person from what they are supposed to be doing for the Kingdom of God. Many people that I have counseled and discipled have struggled because they have opened their minds up to demonic games, books, video games, and movies. Another realm that is very detrimental is horror movies. Bad, tormenting dreams are often a result. These areas are very real door openers to the demonic and the occult. The open doorways here definitely need to be repented of and closed.

One young woman, Mallory, came to me for counseling after suffering for many years. She was experiencing problems spiritually, emotionally, physically, and in her marriage. At the start of our counseling sessions, she filled out a questionnaire that I have all of my counselees complete. As we went through her childhood and history, we were able to pinpoint where the door to the occult was opened.

Mallory remembered seeing the movie "The Craft" as a teenager. That movie had sparked an interest in her and her friends to look into witchcraft. They all desired the power the occult represented and wanted to learn more about how to gain that power. Mallory felt comfortable enough to ask her mother to take her to the nearby witchcraft store. She wanted to get a book about spells. Her mother had taken her to that store previously.

Growing up, Mallory remembers her mother reading books to her about horoscopes, dreams, and stars. She also took her to a palm reader and to a store nearby that specialized in witchcraft.

Her mother was always interested in witchcraft. Mallory's mother, not being a Christian, was unaware of the spiritual ramifications that she and her daughter would face as a result of opening that door.

After Mallory opened the door to the occult through viewing the movie and participated in witchcraft and spells, she began seeing demons, wrote with automatic demonic writing, and played the Ouija board, among other things.

Later, Mallory became a Christian and gave her heart to the Lord, but she struggled and felt defeated as a believer. Coming from a non-Christian home, she had no one to model the Christian faith for her. She didn't understand the importance of reading the Word of God and having a personal relationship with Jesus. She thought that being a good person who believed in Jesus was enough. She told me that true repentance had never happened. She still walked in sin, never surrendering to her life fully to the Lord. In the years following, she tried her best to follow the Lord and just bury all of the past and her involvement with occult activities. Unfortunately, it didn't just go away due to the doors that have been opened to the occult.

When we met, I asked her what had triggered all of the witchcraft being brought back up to the surface. We discovered that it had started a few years earlier after she had accompanied her boss on a trip overseas. While there, the boss introduced Mallory and her co-workers to a family that made honey wine and had a cultural coffee ceremony, which involved tea cup reading, saying this was a common practice in her home country. Mallory unknowingly opened herself up to this demonic practice as she looked into the cup, being ignorant of the spiritual ramifications, she did the reading. It immediately opened her up to seeing the demonic in the spirit, which caused a reactivation of the demonic bondages that Mallory had tried so hard to bury. From that point on, her problems increased and continued for many years.

When we realized this, we prayed and took it to the Lord. She personally denounced all involvement with the occult, repented, and closed all of the doors that had been opened to witchcraft and the occult. These doors were generationally opened to her from her mother and also by Mallory herself when she opened doors to the occult herself. She is completely free now and is a lovely young woman who loves and serves the Lord. She has learned how to walk out her salvation and healing with the Lord and through the Word of God!

In their search for God, many are seeking a way to fill the spiritual void in their lives. They have opened themselves up to the occult, false religion and New Age. Annie was one of these. She tried many pathways in her search for God: New Age, Eastern Religions, Hinduism, had studied Gandhi and astrology, and attended the Burning Man Festivals. When she came to me for counseling, she was desperate to find the pathway to the one true God and be set free from all of the bondages and open doorways in her life. Through the process of counseling, we discovered and closed those doors. The Lord beautifully redeems.

When someone has been involved in the occult, false religion, and new age, it is very important that they shut down their ability to hear from the Lord for some time as they go through the process of sanctification. This is due to the fact that they are accustomed to hearing from the enemy. Often they will confuse the voice of the enemy with God's voice. During this time, they need to hear from the Lord only through the Bible, God's Word.

The person who has participated in occult activities and false religion must confess and renounce these sins, asking the Lord to forgive them, cleanse them, and remove the effects of these sins from their lives. They must close the doors that were opened to the enemy in prayer by the blood and authority of the Lord Jesus Christ. They must sever all ties with people involved in the occult and false religion and get rid of all related literature and paraphernalia. It is also very important for them to pray over their home, cleansing it of all demonic activity. This will give them a firm foundation to start their life in Christ.

The good news is that the Lord can close every door opened to the occult and false religion. He will not only close those doors but beautifully redeem you and restore you.

He Has Good Plans for You

For I know the plans I have for you, declares the Lord, plans to prosper you and not to harm you, plans to give you hope and a future. Then you will call upon me and come and pray to me, and I will listen to you. You will seek me and find me when you seek me with all your heart. I will be found by you, declares the Lord, and will bring you back from captivity (Jeremiah 29:11-14).

The following are some of the lies the enemy uses to get us to open the door and engage in occult activities.

Lies of the Enemy to Get You to Engage in the Occult and False Religion

1. I can watch it or participate in it and it won't affect me. - *Lie* Witchcraft, psychics, tarot cards, New Age, false religion, occult movies and books, etc. all open a door to the enemy.

2. I was forced to watch or listen to that. - *Lie* You have a choice. Say no.

3. It will give me power. I will just try this spell once. - *Lie* It hooks you. Remember anyone or anything that has a power not from God is from the devil.

4. Horoscopes: I can read it because I don't believe it. It won't affect me. - *Lie*

5. I can play that occult video game; it won't bother me. - *Lie* Proverbs 12:11 says: *He who works his land will have abundant food, but he who chases fantasies lacks judgement.*

6. The kids can play with those occult influenced toys; it won't affect their development. - *Lie* Children that play with occult influenced toys, video games, or watch occult influenced cartoons are adversely affected. When it comes time to make a decision about who they will serve, they already have an affinity towards the occult.

7. Occult, New Age, and false religion books: Reading this book won't do anything to me. - *Lie* Many books today have occult, New Age, and false messages and meanings interlaced in their stories. Don't read them or have them in your home!

8. Occult games such as the Ouija board, Magic the Gathering, Pokémon, etc. are just harmless games. They're okay. - *Lie* No they're not! They entice the player deeper into the world of the occult. They open the door.

9. Horror and Occult movies: I can watch them; they won't affect me. - *Lie* In counseling, I have discovered people are tormented with bad dreams, thoughts, and memories as a result of watching horror movies. It is another gateway to get people interested in the occult. The Harry Potter movies have been the largest recruiter to the occult in modern times, unfortunately targeted and marketed towards children.

10. They are just trying to find God in their own way. Let's peacefully co-exist. - *Lie* There is only one way to God, and that is through His Son, Jesus Christ (John 14:6).

Scriptures to Help you to Overcome in the Area of the Occult and False Religion

Let no one be found among you who sacrifices his son or daughter in the fire, who practices divination or sorcery, interprets omens, engages in witchcraft, or casts spells, or who is a medium or spiritist or who consults the dead. Anyone who does these things is detestable to the Lord, and because of these detestable practices the Lord your God will drive out those nations before you (Deut. 18:10-12).

Salvation is found in no one else, for there is no other name under heaven given to men by which we must be saved (Acts 4:12).

But you belong to God, my dear children. You have already won a victory over those people, because the Spirit who lives in you is greater than the spirit who lives in the world (1 John 4:4 NLT).

For the time will come when men will not put up with sound doctrine. Instead to suit their own desires, they will gather around them a great number of teachers to say what their itching ears want to hear. They will turn their ears away from the truth and turn aside to myths (2 Timothy 4:3-4).

For our struggle is not against flesh and blood, but against the rulers, against the authorities, against the powers of this dark world and against the spiritual forces of evil in the heavenly realms (Ephesians 6:12).

How God anointed Jesus of Nazareth with the Holy Spirit and Power, and how He went around doing good and healing all who were under the power of the devil, because God was with Him (Acts 10:38).

For if you wander beyond the teaching of Christ, you will leave God behind; while if you are loyal to Christ's teachings, you will have God too (2 John 9).

The acts of the sinful nature are obvious: sexual immorality, impurity, and debauchery, idolatry and witchcraft; hatred, discord, jealousy, fits of rage, selfish ambition, dissensions, factions and envy, drunkenness, orgies, and the like. I warn you, as I did before, that those who live like this will not inherit the kingdom of God (Galatians 5:19-21).

Abhor what is evil. Cling to what is good (Romans 12:9).

God was displeased when Saul sought the help of a medium: "Saul died because he was unfaithful to the Lord; he did not keep the word of the Lord and even consulted a medium for guidance, and did not inquire of the Lord. So, the Lord put him to death and turned the kingdom over to David son of Jesse" (1 Chronicles 10:13-14).

The Spirit clearly says that in later times some will abandon the faith and follow deceiving spirits and things taught by demons (1 Timothy 4:1).

But, dear friends, remember what the apostles of our Lord Jesus Christ foretold. They said to you, "In the last times there will be scoffers who will follow their own ungodly desires." These are the men who divide you, who follow mere natural instincts and do not have the Spirit (Jude 17-19).

Have nothing to do with the fruitless deeds of darkness, but rather expose them. For it is shameful even to mention what the disobedient do in secret (Ephesians 5:11-12).

Test everything. Hold on to the good. Avoid every kind of evil (1 Thessalonians 5:21-22).

And I solemnly declare to everyone who hears the words of prophecy written in this book: If anyone adds anything to what is written here, God will add to that person the plagues described in this book. And if anyone removes any of the words from this book of prophecy, God will remove that person's share in the tree of life and in the holy city that are described in this book (Revelation 22:18-19 NLT).

My people are destroyed for lack of knowledge (Hosea 4:6).

He said to me: "It is done. I am the Alpha and the Omega, the Beginning and the End. To him who is thirsty I will give to drink without cost from the spring of the water of life. He who overcomes will inherit all this, and I will be his God and he will be my son. But the cowardly, the unbelieving, the vile, the murderers, the sexually immoral, those who practice magic arts, the idolaters and all liars-their place will be in the fiery lake of burning sulfur. This is the second death" (Revelations 21:6-8).

For such men are false apostles, deceitful workmen, masquerading as apostles of Christ. And no wonder, for Satan himself masquerades as an angel of light. It is not surprising then, if his servants masquerade as servants of righteousness. Their end will be what their actions deserve (2 Corinthians 11:13-15).

Once when we were going to the place of prayer, we were met by a slave girl who had a spirit by which she predicted the future. She earned a great deal of money for her owners by fortune-telling. This girl followed Paul and the rest of us, shouting, "These men are servants of the Most High God, who are telling you the way to be saved." She kept this up for many days. Finally, Paul became so troubled that he turned around and said to the spirit, "In the name of Jesus Christ I command you to come out of her!" At that moment the spirit left her (Acts 16:16-18).

You adulterous people, don't you know that friendship with the world is hatred toward God? Anyone who chooses to be a friend of the world becomes an enemy of God (James 4:4).

He who does what is sinful is of the devil, because the devil has been sinning from the beginning. The reason the son of God appeared was to destroy the devil's work (1 John 3:8).

Dear friends, do not believe every spirit, but test the spirits to see whether they are from God, because many false prophets have gone out into the world. This is how you can recognize the Spirit of God; Every spirit that acknowledges that Jesus Christ has come in the flesh is from God, but every spirit that does not acknowledge Jesus is not from God. This is the spirit of the antichrist, which you have heard is coming and even now is already in the world (1 John 4:1-3).

But mark this: There will be terrible times in the last days. People will be lovers of themselves, lovers of money, boastful, proud, abusive, disobedient to their parents, ungrateful, unholy, without love, unforgiving, slanderous, without self-control, brutal, not lovers of the good, treacherous, rash, conceited, lovers of pleasure rather than lovers of God-having a form of godliness but denying the power. Have nothing to do with them (2 Timothy 3:1-5).

Jesus said: I am the way, and the truth, and the life. No one can come to the Father except through me (John 14:6 ESV).

No, in all these things we are more than conquerors through Him who loved us. For I am convinced that neither death nor life, neither angels nor demons, neither the present nor the future, nor any powers, neither height nor depth, nor anything else in all creation, will be able to separate us from the love of God that is in Christ Jesus our Lord (Romans 8:37-39).

Blessed are those who wash their robes, that they may have the right to the tree of life and may go through the gates into the city. Outside are the dogs, those who practice magic arts, the sexually immoral, the murderers, the idolaters, and everyone who loves and practices falsehood (Revelation 22:14-15).

And they overcame him by the blood of the Lamb, and by the word of their testimony and they loved not their lives unto death (Revelation 12:11 KJV).

[1] *The Billy Graham Christian Worker's Handbook*
[2] Christian answers.net

If we confess our sins,
He is faithful and just
to forgive us our sins
and to cleanse us
from all unrighteousness

1 JOHN 1:9

≈6≈

THE PRAYER THAT SETS YOU FREE

He who conceals his sins does not prosper, but whoever confesses and renounces them finds mercy. Blessed is the man who always fears the Lord, he who hardens his heart falls into trouble (Proverbs 28:13-14).

This chapter is about identifying what sins have opened doors to the enemy in your life and how to close those doors. The previous chapters have detailed the four categories of Open Doors: generational sins, sexual immorality, drugs and addiction, and the occult and false religion.

Those who attempt to deny their sins or keep them hidden rather than acknowledge, repent, and forsake them, will not make spiritual progress if the doors to these sins are not closed. They will continually be dealing with these sins and the effects of them in their lives.

Hardening of your heart happens when the Holy Spirit shows you something that is wrong, but you ignore it. It is very important to confess your sins to the Lord. God's forgiveness and mercy are available for all who come to Him in sincere repentance. Repentance is a decision we make. It is made possible by the enabling grace given to us as we hear and believe the Gospel.

If we confess our sins, He is faithful and just to forgive us our sins and to cleanse us from all unrighteousness (1 John 1:9 ESV).

If I had cherished sin in my heart, the Lord would not have listened (Psalm 66:18).

And they overcame him by the Blood of the Lamb and by the word of their testimony, and they did not love their lives to the death (Revelation 12:11 NKJV).

I recommend after reading through the first five chapters and learning about open doors, that you spend some time in prayer. Find a quiet place, go before the Lord, asking Him to show you what doors (sins) that you have opened. On page 70, I have provided a worksheet to help you. Write down each door opener under their particular category: generational sins, sexual immorality, drugs and addiction, and the occult and false religion. You can also refer to page 68-69, where there is a list detailing each category.

Many times, the Lord will bring to remembrance sins and open doors in our lives through a dream or memory. I have counseled many people that have had more than one page of door openers. One session in particular that I remember, took more than three hours of prayer, repentance, and closing the doors. Remember, it doesn't matter if you have just a few doors open or many. What matters is that you close those open doors so that you can move on and live an overcoming, victorious life for the Lord Jesus Christ.

After you have prayerfully completed the list of open doors, go through each section one at a time. It is helpful to say each category and each sin under that category aloud as you pray. Pray and repent, telling the Lord you are sorry. Ask Him to forgive you, cleanse you, and take away any effects of that sin and of opening that door from your life. Then close that door by the blood and authority of Jesus Christ.

Generational Sins: *Including but not limited to* Alcoholism, Drug Addiction, Substance Abuse, Anger, Lying, Stealing, Immorality, Incest, Adultery, Molestation, Pornography, Witchcraft, Voodoo, the Occult, Secret Orders, Masons, Rainbow Girls, De Molay, Job's Daughters, Cults, False Religion, Gangs, Cleansings, Violence, Gambling, Fear, New Age.

Sexual Immorality: *Including but not limited to* Fornication, Adultery, Pornography, Promiscuity, Abortion, Abortion Pill, Morning After Pill, Molestation, Prostitution, Sex trafficking, Child Pornography, Internet Sex Sites, Phone Sex, Hook up Apps, Immoral Movies, Magazines, and Books, Bestiality, Masturbation, Rape, Incest, Lust, Sexual Fantasies, Orgies, Bi-Sexuality, Homosexuality, Lesbian, Trans-Sexual.

Drugs: *Including but not limited to* Alcohol (Alcoholism), Marijuana, (Cannabis), Meth, Crank, (methamphetamine), Barbiturates, LSD (Lysergic Acid Diethylamide), Heroin, Hashish, Opium, Buttons-Mescaline, Cocaine, PCP, Angel Dust, Hallucinogenic Mushrooms-Psilocybin, Anabolic Steroids, gym candy, Crack, Speed, Uppers, Amphetamines, Black Beauties, Hearts, Sedatives, Vaping, Inhaling/Huffing, (Inhalants), Fentanyl, GHB, MDMA, Ecstasy, Ketamine, Buprenorphine, Methadone, Morphine, Benzodiazepines, Phencyclidine, Stimulants, Depressants, Opioids, Oxycodone, (Opiates), misuse of prescription drugs.

Addictions: *Including but not limited to* Alcoholism, Drug Addiction, Substance Abuse, Pornography, Sexual Addictions, Eating Addictions, Anorexia, Bulimia, Video Gaming, Gambling, etc.

The Occult/False Religion: *Including but not limited to* witchcraft, sorcery, black magic, white magic, wicca, psychics, spells, voodoo, tarot cards, horoscopes, astrology, fortune telling, palm readers, tea leaf readings, spiritism, seances, horror movies, Dungeons and Dragons, Ouija board, Magic the Gathering, Harry Potter books and movies, Twilight movies and books, occult movies, books, and video games, Halloween, Pokémon, crystals, chakra, reiki, acupuncture, channeling, cleansings, telepathy, worship of demons, Eastern Religions, New Age, hypnosis, magic arts, occult toys and cartoons, astral projection, clairvoyance, extrasensory perception, transcendental meditation, yoga (most), visualization, the law of attraction.

Note: These lists say including, but not limited to, meaning you may have participated in a sin that is not listed here.

Generational

1.
2.
3.
4.
5.
6.
7.
8.
9.
10.

Occult / False Religion

1.
2.
3.
4.
5.
6.
7.
8.
9.
10.

Drugs & Addiction

1.
2.
3.
4.
5.
6.
7.
8.
9.
10.

Sexual Immorality

1.
2.
3.
4.
5.
6.
7.
8.
9.
10.

The Prayer that Sets You Free

The Closing Doors Prayer

"Dear Lord Jesus, I ask you to forgive me. I repent for opening a door to _____ (name door category).

"For the sins of _____, _____, and _____."
(name each sin in that category).

"Please cleanse me from these sins, and the effects of these sins in my life. I now close these doors, by the blood and authority of the Lord Jesus Christ. Amen."

They overcame him by the blood of the Lamb and by the word of their testimony (Revelation 12:11 NKJV).

They Overcame him
by the *Blood of*
the lamb
and the WORD
of their

Testimony

Revelation 12:11

During counseling, I do the closing doors session with each person. I believe it is helpful to say each category and sin aloud as you repent. You can pray and do this alone with the Lord also.

In the area of generational sins, you are repenting for the sins of those that went before you, closing those open doors and breaking the effects of those sins upon you, your children, and your grandchildren.

Praise God! You are now forgiven and free! The open doorways are closed! The enemy no longer has a legal right to access, affect, and torment you through those doorways.

After you have closed the open doors in your life, use the key principles in the following chapters to learn how to maintain your freedom and walk out your healing. You will learn the keys of how to keep these doors to the enemy closed by guarding your heart, renewing your mind, and retraining your brain. These key principles will enable and empower you to live an overcoming life with the Lord.

Blessed is the one whose transgressions are forgiven; whose sins are covered. Blessed is the one whose sin the Lord does not count against them and in whose spirit is no deceit (Psalm 32:1-2).

See to it that no
one fails to obtain
the grace of God;
that no "root of
bitterness" springs
up and causes trouble.
and by it many become
defiled...

HEBREWS 12:15

⁓7⁓

ROOTS—STRONGHOLDS IN YOUR LIFE

See to it that no one misses the grace of God and that no bitter root grows up to cause trouble and defile many (Hebrews 12:15).

This chapter explains the key to understanding the roots and strongholds that, unfortunately, we all have in our lives. It examines Bible characters and the roots and godly attributes in their lives. It will show you how to examine and pull out the roots in your own life and replace them with godly attributes.

A root is basically a belief system at work in your life. It creates a stronghold and has to be identified, pulled up, broken and destroyed. Roots cause spiritual cancer in your life. In counseling, one of the most important steps is identifying the roots or causes of a problem. Identifying and removing them are an important key to being free and living an overcoming life.

Since roots form your belief system, if you believe something, then a stronghold will grow around that to enforce it. Strongholds are things that have taken root in our lives. Strongholds can be evil actions. They can be things we continually say, think, or dwell upon. That is why roots have to be dug up and the system that made a person believe the stronghold, be dismantled and discredited. For example, a root of bitterness or unforgiveness will cause you to have a stronghold symptom of anger.

If you believe that you are worthless or no good because you were told that as a child, then strongholds that come up will help convince you that you are indeed worthless. Eventually a root of unworthiness will form, which is why we must identify, dismantle, and destroy them. Then new things can grow, and the strongholds are no longer strongholds holding evil to you, but they are attributes holding good to you.

Roots: *Including but not limited to* Unworthiness, Rejection, Fear, Abandonment, Judgement, Bitterness, Unforgiveness, Pride, Rebellion, Hatred, Religious Spirit, Self-Righteousness, Ungratefulness, Addiction, Perversion, Lust, Insecurity, A Need for Power, Condemnation, Self-Condemnation, Narcissism, Vanity, Stubbornness, Selfishness.

Symptoms of Roots: *Including but not limited to* Anger, Control, Guilt, Worry, Shame, Anxiety, Low Self Worth, Remorse, OCD, Disobedience, Depression, Sadness, Feelings of Suicide, Despair, Being Needy, Laziness, No Self Control, Overly Sensitive, Doubt, Offense, Resentment, Manipulation, Deceitfulness, Loneliness, Lying.

For though we walk in the flesh, we do not war after the flesh:
For the weapons of our warfare are not carnal, but mighty
through God to the pulling down of strongholds; casting down
imaginations, and every high thing that exalteth itself against
the knowledge of God, and bringing into captivity every
thought to the obedience of Christ (2 Corinthians 10:3-5 KJV).

Taking our thoughts captive is a very important step in overcoming strongholds. Do not dwell on things that are not of God. Replace bad or negative thoughts with scripture passages. Set your mind to praising Him (Jesus) instead.

A Stronghold Is Two-fold

1. An inner stronghold that holds your thoughts captive.

2. An outer stronghold that forms addictions and bondages in your life.

As a child I experienced rejection, which caused me to view the world through a lens of rejection and allowed strongholds to develop in my life. I had been serving the Lord for many years, very active in my church, leading women's ministry, prayer ministry, and women's retreats. One day two trusted friends came to me and said, "I think there is something in your life that is a bit off." Not being able to put a finger on what exactly it was, I remember responding to my friends that I did not want anything in my life that was not of God. I decided to set aside the coming weekend to spend it entirely with the Lord, seeking His face and finding out what root had grown in my life that was not of the Lord.

As I sequestered myself in my room to seek the Lord, He allowed me to see myself without the blood of Jesus covering me—not a pretty picture, I can assure you. I was in what I would call a desert place, a place of brokenness before the Lord. The horror of seeing my sins without the blood of Jesus covering them led me to a place of deep repentance. As I was crying and repenting for my sins, my husband Allen came in. I will never forget him patting me on the back as I knelt praying, trying to comfort me saying, "You're not a bad person." I responded back to him emphatically, "Yes, I am! Please leave!" I was seeing myself without the blood of Jesus covering my sins.

From there the Lord brought two different memories to my mind, one from my childhood and one from my teenage years.

In the first memory, I was around twelve years old. My parents were in the middle of a divorce. I was not raised in a Christian home. My parents loved me and my brothers but did not understand the importance of protecting their children spiritually. They believed in God, but He did not have a place of importance in their lives or in our home.

One night my grandmother (on my father's side) was visiting us and a big fight between my parents erupted. Their marriage was disintegrating, and my mother was in the middle of a mental breakdown. My father was trying his best to hold the family together but was not able to. I remember my mother being out of control, yelling at my dad. As dad left to take my grandmother home, she passed by me and said, "And you! You're just like your mother!" Not exactly a compliment! It was directed at me, her granddaughter. Immediately a root of rejection was placed into my soul. The enemy is good at placing roots into our lives when we are young and not under a Christian covering. Children whose parents divorce, many times develop a root of rejection.

The next memory the Lord brought to mind was when I was sixteen. My parents were divorced by then, and my father had remarried. We were on a family vacation at a lake. One night I went into the kitchen of the cabin to get a glass of water. My dad and stepmom were in their room next to the kitchen with the door open. I overheard my stepmother saying how she enjoyed my brothers and thought they were great. Then she said of me, "Well, Caryn, she's getting better." Another root of rejection hit my heart and soul.

What I didn't understand was how these roots of rejection would affect my life. I viewed the world through a lens of rejection. It made me overly sensitive. I cared so much about what everyone else thought of me. I also had developed controlling behaviors in some areas of my life. When I saw this, I asked the Lord, "Lord, I hear your voice, why didn't You show me this sooner?" He then responded to me, "It wasn't time. Now it is."

The Lord wanted me to go forward in healing and wholeness, not viewing life through a lens of rejection. I did not want anything in my life or heart that was not of God.

I quickly made an appointment with my friends and shared with them what the Lord had shown me. We had a time of prayer, pulling out the roots of rejection from my life and placing into my heart the Lord's answer to the world's rejection, which is His love and acceptance.

> *You were taught, with regard to your former way of life, to put off your old self, which is being corrupted by its deceitful desires; to be made new in the attitude of your minds; and to put on the new self, created to be like God in true righteousness and holiness* (Ephesians 4:22-24).

I was set free to see life without that lens of rejection. I was free to live my life and do ministry without that bondage holding me back. Can you imagine? I would never have been able to do my job as a counselor if I had been so concerned with what others thought of me. Now I do what the Lord has set before me, concerned about what He thinks of me and obedient to Him and the cross of Christ.

I always instruct everyone I counsel to take note of the memories the Lord will bring up during this time. It is a valuable resource that helps you to realize what roots and strongholds you are dealing with.

Another area I always delve into is their "ECM" or earliest childhood memory. I ask counselees to think back and tell me the earliest memory they can remember. Many times, this memory has keys into their belief system about themselves, either good or not so good. You can often determine roots and strongholds from this memory.

As a parent, if you notice your children developing a root of fear or rejection, or if you see any other root developing in their lives, you have the authority and spiritual right as their parent to remove and pull out that root in prayer, replacing it with the godly attribute. You would do this gently or even while they are sleeping. For example when pulling out a root of fear in your child's life, you would replace it with the godly attribute of His love (1 John 4:18).

Let's look at some Bible characters for example, such as Esther and Paul. What if Esther had let a root of fear hold her back and kept her from going boldly into the king's presence?

> *Go, gather together all the Jews who are in Susa, and fast for me. Do not eat or drink for three days, night or day. I and my maids will fast as you do. When this is done, I will go to the King, even though it is against the law. And if I perish, I perish* (Esther 4:16).

If Esther had a root of fear, what would have happened to the people of God?

Or let's look at Paul. What if after his conversion to Christianity, he had not taken three years to prepare before doing the ministry to which the Lord had called him to? (See Galatians 1:11-24.) I'm sure he dealt with the roots in his life, or he would not have been able to preach the Gospel of Christ so boldly. After all, he had participated in persecuting Christians and even condoning their deaths. Now, he was going to preach to them?

Zondervan's Bible Dictionary says of Paul's stay in Arabia,

> Paul's visit to Arabia, mentioned in Galatians 1:17, seems best placed between Acts 9:22 and 23. There is no hint that its purpose was to preach; rather it seems that he felt it necessary to retire to rethink his beliefs in the light of the new revelation that had come to him. The exact length of his stay is not certain, but Paul came out of Arabia with the essentials of his theology fixed.

The enemy would definitely have used those things in Paul's life to hold him back in ministry. Just think how many books in the New Testament would not have been written.

Roots and strongholds in our lives have to be identified and pulled out. After they have been identified, ask the Lord to remove them from your life in prayer. Pull out the destructive root(s) and replace it with the attributes of what God intended to be there in the first place.

After the roots have been identified, it is a good idea to do a Bible Word Study on each root (see chapter 9) and the opposite of that root, a godly attribute. For example, if one of your roots is pride, you would study that, and the opposite godly attribute, humility. This helps you to understand that root and to implement ways to remove it from your life, adding the godly attribute in its place. It would then be helpful to study Bible characters (see chapter 9) who had pride in their lives along with those who lived their lives in humility. Memorizing Scriptures that pertain to these areas are a good idea too.

Bible Characters—Roots and Attributes

Joseph—forgiveness, rejection, endurance, hope, patience, leader.

Joseph's brothers—jealousy, rejection, envy, hatred, bitterness, lying, deception.

Esther—identity, lack of fear, obedience, humility.

Daniel—obedience, trust, lack of fear, pure heart, faithfulness, prayer.

Shadrack, Meshack, Abednego—trust, lack of fear, identity.

Gideon—worshiper, his fear turned into worship, he heard and obeyed God.

Jonah—disobedience, rebellion, anger, lack of trust.

Anna—obedience, patience, promises, perseverance, was not afraid to suffer.

Cain—envy, unforgiveness, bitterness, downcast, anger, murder, jealousy.

Abel—forgiving, tenderhearted, faith, dedication.

Samson—pride, vanity, lust, rebellion, not heeding Nazarite vow.

Hannah—prayer, faith, perseverance, persistence.

Deborah—justice, leadership, wisdom, fearless, obedience.

Moses—rejection, identity issues, anger, fellowship with God, leadership.

Samuel—obedience, willing to do difficult things, fearless, leader, not afraid to be influential.

Mary (mother of Jesus)—obedience, faith, believed God, purity, trust.

Ehud—obedient in spite of handicap, fearless, unselfish.

King Saul—jealousy, pride, anger, disobedience, used witchcraft.

Job—perseverance, refused to be influenced, strength.

Ruth—loyal, obedience, left idols behind, willing to see God's plan.

Joshua—courage, obedience, warrior.

Note: This is an example of some of the Bible characters you can study. As you study them, the Lord will show you more attributes and roots in their lives, good and bad, that they had.

The following was written by Samantha. She struggled with a root of unworthiness her entire life. As she went through the biblical counseling process, the Lord gave her this beautiful vision:

Based on the scriptures, John 8:3-11, many of us know the story of the woman caught in adultery. A lot of people focus on what Jesus said to the people: "If any one of you is without sin, let him be the first to throw a stone at her." In the vision, the Lord took me to a place I did not expect.

The scene was brutal. I was the woman guilty, running from the people who despised me. Running for my very life. With no hope of escape and no hope for my life. But then...I was before Jesus. The people who had been chasing me surrounded me. They wanted justice. They were yelling. They wanted blood!

Jesus was there, quiet, gentle and composed. I was collapsed on the ground. Just waiting for the justice, I knew I deserved. Then I heard Jesus speak to the crowd: "Let him who is without sin cast the first stone." The crowd left and I was alone with the Lord. Then He asked me. "Where are your accusers? Is there anyone left here to condemn you?" At this point something happened that revealed a truth about myself. He showed me that I was pointing a finger at myself! He then said: 'Then, neither do I condemn you.'

Then is a very important word here. We must get to the "then" The Lord showed me that due to a root of unworthiness I had been judging and condemning myself for many years.

Judge not, and you will not be judged; condemn not and you will not be condemned; forgive, and you will be forgiven (Luke 6: 37 ESV)

Do these truths only apply to others and not to ourselves? If Jesus doesn't condemn us, why should we condemn ourselves? If we continue to chain ourselves with our own judgments, condemnation, and unforgiveness, how will we ever really be free? Pray and ask Jesus today how to let go of self-condemnation and be free! Because the truth is, in Christ we are no longer condemned.

So now there is no condemnation for those who belong to Christ Jesus (Romans 8:1 NLT).

Feeling as if they will never be worthy enough to be used by the Lord in ministry has held many people back. The Lord showed me many years ago that worthiness is determined after the fact.

How you use the gifts He has given you is what is important.

I want to encourage you to examine and remove the roots and strongholds in your life, then you will be truly free to walk in the Lord's abundance in your life as an overcomer in Him.

Therefore, as you received Christ Jesus the Lord, so walk in Him, having been firmly rooted and now built up in Him and established in your faith. Just as you were instructed, and over-flowing with gratitude (Colossians 2:6-7 NASB)

Scriptures: Genesis 50:20; Psalm 34:4-5, 139:23-24; Proverbs 15:1, 29:11; Matthew 11:28-30; Luke 6:37; John 4:1-26, 8:3-11; Romans 8:12, and chapter 8; 2 Corinthians 5:17,10:3-5; Galatians 1:11-24; Ephesians 4:22-24, 4:26; Philippians 1:6, 4:13; Colossians 2:6-7, 3:8; Hebrews chapter 11, 12:15; James 1:19-20; 1 Peter 5:7; 1 John 4:16; Revelation 12:11.

⚏8⚏

GUARDING YOUR HEART

Above all else, guard your heart, for it is the wellspring of life (Proverbs 4:23).

Above all else, Proverbs says, *guard your heart.* Strong words, *above all else.* I believe that guarding our hearts is one of the most important things we can do. This chapter will show us the importance in today's world of how we need to guard our hearts. Guarding our hearts is of utmost importance!

Two other versions of the Bible translate this verse as:

Keep thy heart with all diligence; for out of it are the issues of life (KJV).

Keep your heart with all vigilance, for from it flow the springs of life (ESV).

The heart is the wellspring of desire and decision. When the Bible speaks of the heart, it is not referring to the physical organ that pumps out blood to every part of the body, but the heart is used in the Bible to refer to our mind, will, and emotions.

We can be sure that failing to guard our hearts will result in a diminishing desire for God and His Kingdom. It will also result in compromise and lukewarmness. If the wellspring of our heart is polluted, it will affect everything else in our lives: our relationships with others, such as our spouse, our family, friends, and most certainly, our relationship with the Lord.

To watch over and guard our hearts above all else will result in a steady, firm walk with the Lord. How do we do this? Let's look at the verses following the admonition to guard our hearts in scripture:

Above all else, guard your heart, for it is the wellspring of life. Put away perversity from your mouth; keep corrupt talk far from your lips. Let your eyes look straight ahead, fix your gaze directly before you, Make level paths for your feet and take only ways that are firm. Do not swerve to the right or the left; Keep your foot from evil (Proverbs 4:23-27).

This is a wonderful prescription from the Word of God as to how we are to walk as a Christian.

How Do We Guard Our Hearts?

We guard our heart by being careful of what we take in through our eyes and ears—what we see and hear. Some would call them our eye gates and ear gates that guard what we say and do and think.

Guarding What We See and Hear

Our eyes: What we view through television, talk shows, books, magazines, newspapers, advertisements, pictures, videos, movies, news, apps, computers, websites, phones, and social media: YouTube, Facebook, Twitter, Snap Chat, Instagram, etc.

Our ears: What we listen to through worldly music, worldly radio talk shows and news, podcasts, and all types of conversation that might include: gossip, perverse talk, negative talk, cussing, etc.

Think about it. It is really hard to overcome the open door of sexual immorality if all you are listening to every day is hip hop, country, or hard rock songs that are full of sexual references, not to mention lying, cheating, drugs, and drinking. There are many songs in every music genre that are full of bad language, violence, sexual immorality, drinking, drugs, cheating, and lying. Basically, these songs are about doing everything against what the Word of God, the Bible, says. How can we fill our hearts with that and expect to walk a pure life? Listening to these songs is certainly not guarding our hearts.

Turn my heart toward your statutes and not toward selfish gain. Turn my eyes away from worthless things; preserve my life according to your word (Psalm 119:36-37).

One time, I was counseling Christine, who was struggling with a life-dominating sin in the area of gambling. Remember, a life-dominating sin is one that controls every aspect of your life. I asked her what she was watching on television. She proceeded to list off a string of reality TV shows and sitcoms that were full of sexual immorality, swearing, vulgar talk, and other immoral situations. I explained to her that she could not fill her mind and heart with that vulgarity and expect to live in a Christ-like manner.

I shared with her Galatians 6:7-8 which says: *Do not be deceived: God cannot be mocked. A man reaps what he sows. The one who sows to please his sinful nature, from that nature will reap destruction; the one who sows to please the Spirit, from the Spirit will reap eternal life.*

"Think of it," I said, "What are you feeding: your spiritual man or your sinful nature?" She said to me: "You can't be asking me to give up my TV?" I responded, "The choice is yours. But I am telling you that you can't sow to the flesh and expect to reap the Spirit."

I'm sad to say that she did not complete her counseling and is still struggling with her sin today. Why? Because she would not give up immoral television and sowing to her flesh, her sinful nature. You cannot live an overcoming life and be constantly filling yourself up with things that are not of God.

Guarding What We Say

We also guard our hearts by watching what we say. Proverbs 4:25 says: *Put away perversity from your mouth; keep corrupt talk far from your lips.*

> *Do not let any unwholesome talk come out of your mouths, but only what is helpful for building others up according to their needs, that it may benefit those who listen* (Ephesians 4:29).

The Lord taught me through this verse many years ago that not only was I supposed stop saying bad or harmful things, but I was to ask Him, through prayer, what He would like to say through me to whomever I was talking. It is so beautiful to use this way of talking to edify and lift up our family, friends, and those we minister to.

TWAs—Thoughts, Words, and Actions

Jesus talks of the heart in Mark 7:20-23. In verses 20-23, He says:

> *What comes out of a man is what makes him unclean. For from within, out of men's hearts, come evil thoughts, sexual immorality, theft, murder, adultery, greed, malice, deceit, lewdness, envy, slander, arrogance and folly. All these evils come from inside and make a man unclean.*

Jesus said that what makes a man unclean are the sins that stem from the heart. These sins spiritually defile a person. An impure heart will defile and corrupt one's thoughts, words, and actions. In counseling I call this your TWAs—thoughts, words, and actions. Every day it is good to do a check and see if your thoughts, words, and actions are pure and lining up with the Word of God.

Taking every thought captive means bringing all of your thoughts into alignment with Christ's will. Failure to do so will lead to immorality and eventually spiritual death (2 Corinthians 10:5, Psalm 51, Romans 6:16, 6:23, 8:13).

Don't Harden Your Heart

Failure to guard your heart, a refusal to listen to the Holy Spirit, and disobeying what God commands in the Bible, will eventually result in your heart being hardened. An example of this in the Bible is Pharaoh's heart at the time of the exodus (Exodus 7:3-14:17). We are warned as believers against hardening our hearts.

They are darkened in their understanding and separated from the life of God because of the ignorance that is in them due to the hardening of their hearts. Having lost all sensitivity, they have given themselves over to sensuality so as to indulge in every kind of impurity, with a continual lust for more (Ephesians 4:18-19).

In Hebrews 3:8-12, verse 12 cautions: *See to it, brothers, that none of you has a sinful, unbelieving heart that turns away from the living God.*

Blessed is the man who always fears the Lord, but he who hardens his heart falls into trouble (Proverbs 28:14).

As water reflects a face, so man's heart reflects the man (Proverbs 27:19).

Guarding What We Think

It is of utmost importance to guard what we think about, taking every thought captive and making it obedient to Jesus Christ (2 Corinthians 10:5). Remember, sin starts with a thought, then we entertain it, then we act on it. We can stop this progression by taking captive every thought! Guarding what we think about is key to keeping our minds pure. Failure to guard what we think about will result in a departure from the paths of safety and the way of the Lord. Philippian 4:8 instructs us what to think about: *Whatever is **true**, whatever is **noble**, whatever is **right**, whatever is **pure**, whatever is **lovely**, whatever is **admirable**—if anything is excellent or **praiseworthy**—think about such things* (my emphasis).

Guarding What We Do

I love Psalm 24. Let's look at verses 3-5:

Who may ascend the hill of the Lord? Who may stand in His holy place? He who has clean hands and a pure heart, who does not lift up his soul to an idol or swear by what is false. He will receive blessing from the Lord and vindication from God his Savior.

The psalmist here is emphasizing that those who want to serve God and receive His blessing must be pursuing a pure heart and a righteous life. They must keep the Lord first in their lives in all they do. Clean hands are hands that are free from external acts of sin. A pure heart refers to inward holiness and right motives. Only the pure in heart will see God (Matthew 5:8).

Also, Proverbs instructs us to: *Make level paths for your feet, and take only ways that are firm, do not swerve to the right or the left; keep your foot from evil* (Proverbs 4:26-27).

We must fix our gaze upon Jesus, looking directly ahead and not looking to the left or right, not getting distracted by the things of this world. Keeping our feet from evil.

Guarding what we say, what we see, what we hear, what we think, and what we do, all play a very important part in guarding our hearts. To watch over and guard our hearts above all else will result in a steady, firm walk with the Lord. This is definitely a critical key to living a free and overcoming life.

Scriptures: Exodus 7:3-14:17; Jeremiah 17:9; Psalm 24, 25, 51, 66:18, 119:1-2, 119:11, 119:36-37; Proverbs 4:23-27, 6:6-8, 17:3, 27:19, 28:14; Matthew 5:8; Mark 7:14-23; Luke 6:45; Romans 6: 16, 6:23, 8:13; 2 Corinthians 10:5; Galatians 6:7-8; Ephesians 4:18-19, 29-31; Hebrews 3:8-12; James 4:7-8; 1 John 3:21-24.

I have hidden your word in my heart, that I might not sin against you.

Psalm119:11

OVERCOMING SIN WITH SCRIPTURE

The Bible has the answers to all of our problems, especially in the area of how to overcome sin with scripture. Learn how to overcome the sin in your life with the Word of God. God's Word has transforming power. It gives you the power to overcome sin. It helps you to renew your mind (see chapter 10), and to overcome bad habits (see chapter 11).

This chapter will show you how to overcome sin with scripture, which is a necessary key to living an overcoming life.

Let's look at Hebrews 4:12:

For the Word of God is living and active. Sharper that any double-edged sword, it penetrates even to dividing soul and spirit, joints and marrow; it judges the thoughts and attitudes of the heart.

God's Word is truly living and active. It is often referred to as a double-edged sword: it brings healing and life to those who submit to it in faith. It can also pronounce judgment on those who disregard it. Because His Word is living and active, it has the ability to penetrate our hearts and minds.

God's Word also contains the spiritual principles that will help you to avoid many sorrows, pitfalls, and tragedies brought on by wrong decisions and choices. I encourage you to treasure its wisdom, love it, and steadfastly hold on to its precepts in all of life's situations.

God's Word—Our Weapon to Fight With

As we read, study, memorize and apply scripture to our lives, we learn how to overcome sin. The Word of God is the sword of the Spirit. Ephesians 6:17 says: *Take the helmet of salvation and the sword of the Spirit, which is the Word of God.* The Word of God is our offensive weapon. It is how we fight off the enemy. Jesus Himself fought the devil with scripture:

Then Jesus was led by the Spirit into the wilderness to be tempted there by the devil. For forty days and forty nights he fasted and became very hungry. During that time the devil came and said to him, "If you are the Son of God, tell these stones to become loaves of bread." But Jesus told him, "No! The Scriptures say, 'People do not live by bread alone, but by every word that comes from the mouth of God.' Then the devil took him to the holy city, Jerusalem, to the highest point of the temple, and said, "If you are the Son of God, jump off! For the scriptures say, He will order his angels to protect you. And they will hold you up with their hands so you won't even hurt your foot on a stone." Jesus responded, "The Scriptures also say, You must not test the Lord, your God."

Next the devil took him to peak of a very high mountain and showed Him all the kingdoms of the world and their glory. "I will give it all to you," he said, "if you will kneel down and worship me." "Get out of here, Satan" Jesus told him. "For the scriptures say, You must worship the Lord your God and serve only Him." Then the devil went away, and angels came and took care of Jesus (Matthew 4:1-11 NLT).

Note: Luke 4:13 says: *When the devil had finished tempting Jesus, he left Him until the next opportunity came.*

Notice how Satan manipulated scripture to serve his needs, to tempt Jesus to disobey the will of God in his life. That is exactly why we must know scripture and use the discernment given to us by the Holy Spirit. The enemy takes scripture out of context and uses half-truths. The enemy is still doing the same today, trying to deceive believers. That is why we must always let scripture interpret scripture by reading it in context and looking at the scriptures before and after the passage, in order to interpret it.

In teaching *Foundations of Faith, Session Two, The Bible*, I always do an object lesson. I use a machete and a butter knife. (Who wants to come to that class? Ha ha!) I tell the students,

> This is what you are fighting the enemy off with, either a butter knife or a machete. What weapon you have to use depends on how much scripture you put into your life. According to Ephesians 6:17, the Word of God is the sword of the Spirit. Big knife, a lot of the Word. Little knife, a little Word. If you seem to have a lot of problems fighting off the enemy, my guess is you have a little butter knife to fight with.

But it doesn't have to be that way. You have the Sword of the Spirit available to you! The Bible is your offensive weapon. If you know the Word, and how to apply it to your life, you will be less likely to sin. Some use the Bible only after they have sinned, in an effort to recover from the effect of that sin. We need to know what the Word of God says to keep us from committing the sin in the first place!

Three Helpful Ways to Use the Bible to Overcome Sin

I always recommend that the way to overcome sin with scripture is through Bible study. There are three basic types of study to do this: Bible memory verses, Scripture word studies, and Bible character studies. It is hard, or nearly impossible, to change ourselves, no matter how hard we try. But with the help of Jesus, the Holy Spirit, and the Bible, we can change.

Bible Memory Verses

I have hidden your Word in my heart that I might not sin against you (Psalm 119:11).

Pick out a Bible scripture to memorize that deals with the particular sin you are struggling to overcome. I recommend printing it out on a 3x5 card. Include the scripture and reference. Carry it around with you, looking at it many times throughout the day. Soon you will have the verse committed to memory, and the Lord will remind you of them as needed. Ask yourself: "What does that verse mean to me?" and "How am I going to apply it to my life?" For example, if you are struggling to overcome temptation, you would memorize:

No temptation has overtaken you but such as is common to man; and God is faithful, who will not allow you to be tempted beyond what you are able, but with the temptation will provide the way of escape also, so that your will be able to endure it (1 Corinthians 10:13 NASB).

You can also look up the verse in different Bible versions such as: ESV, KJV, NKJV, NASB, NLT, or AMP. You can use Bible Gateway online for this tool. Looking the verse up in different versions will help you to get a deeper understanding of it.

Scripture Word Studies

All scripture is God-breathed and is useful for teaching, rebuking, correcting and training in righteousness, so that the man (or woman) of God may be thoroughly equipped for every good work (2 Timothy 3:16-17).

Pick out a word you would like to study, such as *forgive*. This might be an area you are struggling in or a particular topic in the Bible you want to learn more about. Then do a study on that word. I recommend first looking up the dictionary definition of that particular word.

1. Definition. "Forgive": to give up resentment against or the desire to punish; pardon (an offense or offender); to let go; to cancel a debt. Write the definition out on a paper or I recommend keeping a Bible notebook.

2. Then look up the word forgive in the Bible, using a concordance or go online to Bible Gateway.com. For instance, in the Bible, using the concordance in the back, go to the word "forgive." Pick out the scriptures that stand out to you the most. Look them up and write them out. You should have at least ten to fifteen scriptures.

3. Then you would write several paragraphs on what the Bible says about the word, why you should forgive and live a life of forgiveness, and how you will apply forgiveness to your life. It is also good to study the opposite—unforgiveness—using scriptures to explain what happens to those who carry unforgiveness in their lives.

Remember, we do not care about someone else's opinion on forgiveness. You should be concerned about only what the Bible says about it, what the Holy Spirit is showing you, and how you personally are going to apply it to your life.

Some Bible Word study ideas might be: lying, fear, gossip, bad language, discord, anxiety, worry, lack of self-control, pride, etc. or: faith, love, peace, joy, patience, kindness, forgiveness, wisdom, discernment, blameless, pure heart, holiness, humility, etc.

Bible Character Studies

Pick out a Bible character you would like to study. Maybe they have an attribute you want to work on, such as Joseph and forgiveness, or maybe a Bible character with an attribute you need to work to eliminate in your life, such as Samson and pride. After you have chosen one, read all about their life in the Bible. You can use a Bible dictionary as a tool also, but remember no one else's opinion, just what the Bible and the Holy Spirit are showing you about that person.

For instance: Joseph and forgiveness. Look at the life of Joseph (see Genesis 37-50) and how he continually forgave, over and over again. What was the end result of forgiveness in his life? What would have happened to him if he chose not to forgive and carried unforgiveness, bitterness, or anger in his heart? What speaks to you about the life of Joseph? How can you apply the things that you have learned of his life to yours? What were the effects of forgiveness in his life? Then write a paper about Joseph's life. It should be at least one or two pages long. In chapter 7—Roots, Strongholds in Your Life, there is a list of Bible characters, their roots, and godly attributes in their lives for you to study.

Develop a Bible study plan. Using a notebook, list the sins or bad habits you want to eliminate—"put off"—from your life. Then list out the godly attributes you want to add—"put on"—in your life. Look up scriptures or sections of scriptures that correspond to those lists. Write them out, then study them, selecting favorites to memorize. Look up and study Bible characters who have these attributes. Write a paper on these Bible characters using the instructions in this chapter. Doing these three things: Bible Memory Verses, Scripture Word Studies, and Bible Character Studies will help you to become an overcomer and mature in your faith.

Note: *Please take the Discipleship Quiz in the Appendix. The test will help you to determine which areas of your life to work on.*

Important Ways to Fight Sin with Scripture

The following ten points are some other important ways to fight sin with scripture. By incorporating these attributes and principles into your life you will strengthen your walk with Christ. Knowing them will help you to overcome sin with the Word of God.

1. Wisdom for Daily Living

I recommend reading one chapter of Proverbs per day each month. There are 31 chapters in the book of Proverbs, so that works out perfectly. The book of Proverbs is wisdom for daily living. We all need that!

2. Be a Doer of the Word

Do not merely listen to the Word and so deceive yourselves. Do what it says (James 1:22).

If you spend time reading the Word but not doing it, it does you no good. You merely deceive yourself. We have to implement what we have read and heard from the Word into our lives. Ask the Holy Spirit to help you apply what you have read in the Bible to your life. Become a doer of the Word!

Scriptures: James 1:22-25; Romans 10:17; Hebrews 5:14; Psalm 19:9-11; 2 Timothy 3:16-17.

3. How to Live in Christ

Since, then, you have been raised with Christ, set your hearts on things above, where Christ is seated at the right hand of God. Set your minds on things above, not on earthly things. For you died, and your life is now hidden with Christ in God. When Christ, who is your life, appears, then you also will appear with Him in glory.

Put to death, therefore, whatever belongs to your earthly nature: sexual immorality, impurity, lust, evil desires and greed, which is idolatry. Because of these, the wrath of God is coming. You used to walk in these ways, in the life you once lived. But now you must rid yourselves of all such things as these: anger, rage, malice, slander, and filthy language from your lips. Do not lie to each other, since you have taken off your old self with its practices and have put on the new self, which is being renewed in knowledge in the image of its Creator...

Therefore, as God's chosen people, holy and dearly loved, clothe yourselves with compassion, kindness, humility, gentleness, and patience. Bear with each other and forgive whatever grievances you may have against one another. Forgive as the Lord forgave you. And over all these virtues put on love, which binds them all together in perfect unity.

Let the peace of Christ rule in your hearts, since as members of one body you were called to peace. And be thankful. Let the Word of Christ dwell in you richly as you teach and admonish one another with all wisdom, and as you sing psalms, hymns and spiritual songs with gratitude in your hearts to God. And whatever you do, whether in word or deed, do it all in the name of the Lord Jesus, giving thanks to God the Father through Him (Colossians 3:1-17).

This is one of my favorite sections of scripture! There's so much good information here that will help you to know how to live in Christ, such as setting your mind on things above, not on earthly things; what to put to death from your sinful nature, and what to put on as a believer, so you can live a holy life. It is essential to let the Word of Christ dwell in you richly, and whatever you do, whether in word or deed, do it all in the name of the Lord Jesus, giving thanks to God the Father through Him.

4. Forgiveness

A powerful parable in Matthew 18:21-35, the parable of the unmerciful servant, paints a picture of forgiveness that is impossible to forget. It shows us if we do not forgive, we will not be forgiven by God either. You see, the key to forgiveness is to know we do not have the ability in ourselves (the capacity in our own flesh) to forgive, but Jesus, through us, can and will.

The key to forgiveness is to pray and tell the Lord that you choose to forgive. Then ask Him to come and help you to forgive. For example: "Lord, I choose to forgive "Matthew." Please Lord, come and help me to forgive him."

Bear with each other and forgive whatever grievances you may have against one another. Forgive as the Lord forgave you (Colossians 3:13).

Humility is visible evidence of a repentant person. The humble heart will quickly apologize, and in repentance, seek to change and make amends. A humble person also tends to recognize his shortcomings and is open to receive additional insight. God instructs and teaches His ways to the humbly repentant person.[1]

Most people, who have a problem with forgiveness, choose not to forgive. They choose instead to hold on to unforgiveness, letting that unforgiveness grow into bitterness, rage, and anger. This gives the enemy a foothold in their lives. If you fail to deal biblically with your anger, increasing disobedience to scripture is inevitable. God forgives us our sins when we repent. He cancels our debt. We are to forgive others, who do us wrong, in the same way.

Scriptures: Psalm 103:10-12; Proverbs 16:18-19, 32, 19:19, 29:22-23; Matthew 6:14-15, 18:21-35; Romans 12:14-21; 1 Corinthians 13:4-6; Ephesians 4:26-27, 31-32; Colossians 1:13-14, 3:13; Hebrews 12:14-15; James 1:19-20; 1 Peter 2:23; 1 John 1:9.

5. Love the Word of God

Psalm 119 is a beautiful psalm that teaches us a love for the Word of God. It shows God's Word as a promise, precept, guide, wisdom, teaching, and truth. Read this Psalm to develop a love for God's Word. You can also pray for the Lord to give you a love for His Word and to help you to apply it to your life.

Your Word is a lamp to my feet and a light for my path (Psalm 119:105).

I have hidden your Word in my heart, that I might not sin against you (Psalm 119:11).

How can we see where we are going and what we are to do without scripture, without His Word being a lamp to our feet and a light to our path? How can we avoid sin and the traps of the enemy if we do not know what the Word of God says?

Verse 2 in Psalm 119 says: *Blessed are they who keep his statutes and seek him with all their hearts.* If we as believers, would just follow this verse, what a difference that would make!

6. The Ten Commandments

I am often surprised by the amount of people who do not know the Ten Commandments in Exodus 20:1-20. It is so important to know what God expects of us. Knowing and obeying these commandments will help to keep you from sinning.

1. **You shall have no other gods before me.** God deserves the first place in your life.
2. **You shall not make for yourself an idol.** An idol is anything you put before God.
3. **You shall not use God's name in vain.** Swearing by His name, cussing.
4. **Remember the Sabbath day and keep it holy.** Going to church,

resting, concentrating on the things concerning eternity.

5. **Honor your father and mother.** Treat your parents with honor and respect.

6. **Do not murder.** You are not God; you don't get to decide if someone lives or dies. (For example: abortion).

7. **Do not commit adultery.** Honor your marriage vows before God.

8. **Do not steal.** Don't take things that are not yours.

9. **Do not give false testimony.** Don't lie. Speak the truth.

10. **Do not covet.** Don't want things that are not yours.

The first four commandments deal with our relationship to God—vertical. The last six commandments deal with our relationships with others—horizontal.

7. The Power and Authority of the Name of Jesus

Therefore, God elevated him to the place of highest honor and gave him the name above all other names, that at the name of Jesus every knee should bow, in heaven and on earth and under the earth, and every tongue declare that Jesus Christ is Lord, to the glory of God the Father (Philippians 2:9-11).

One of the most important things we should never forget is that Jesus has paid a huge price for us to be able to walk in His authority. 1 Peter 1:18-19 says:

For you know that it was not with perishable things such as silver or gold that you were redeemed from the empty way of life handed down to you from your forefathers, but with the precious blood of Christ, a lamb without blemish or defect.

Many times, though, we live below that level of power and authority. At church we call this "living below the bloodline." As a son or daughter of God, we have the privilege and right to use His name and authority.

103

There is power and authority in the name of Jesus, and there is power in the blood of Jesus, shed on the cross of Christ. There is power to heal the sick, deliver the oppressed, and set the captives free (Mark 16:15-18). We fight the enemy in the name of Jesus and by His blood that was shed for us.

Jesus has promised us as believers that His presence, authority, and power will accompany us as we push back the darkness with the light of Jesus Christ.[2]

And they overcame him by the blood of the lamb and the word of their testimony, and they did not love their lives to the death (Revelation 12:11 NKJV)

Scriptures: Isaiah 53:1-5; Matthew 10:1-16, 16:23, 28:18-20; Hebrews 9:11-10:18; 1 Corinthians 11:23-26; Luke 10:1-20, 24:47-49; 1 Peter 1:18-19, 2:24; Philippians 2:9-11; 1 John 1:7; Revelation 12:11.

8. Not Submitting to Fear, Worry, and Anxiety

Cast all of your cares upon Him, for He cares for you (1 Peter 5:7)

Worry and anxiety can be overcome as you develop your trust in God, trusting Him for all things and in all circumstances. The terms worry and anxiety can cover a wide range of problems, resulting most of the time from unfounded fears. The most important things you can do is take captive every thought (2 Corinthians 10:5); keep your thoughts trained on His Word; and what is true, noble, right, pure, lovely, admirable, excellent or praiseworthy (Philippians 4:8); and use Philippians 4:4-7 as a prescription to fight worry.

Make sure you are spending enough time in the Word and in prayer. Limiting your news intake can also be helpful. Keeping your eyes and lives centered on the Lord and His Word, will cause the cares and worries of this world to fade away. Trust the Lord to take care of you (Proverbs 3:5-6). Fear is a root (see chapter 7) and must be taken out of your life. To overcome worry and anxiety, you must retrain your thinking. (see chapter 11) and become full of the Word of God.

Never will I leave you or forsake you (Hebrews 13:5b).

Remember God has promised us His presence (Hebrews 13:5b), His provision (Psalm 37:5), and His protection (Psalm 91). Ask the Lord to fill you with His love, that you would see through His eyes and feel with His heart. It is important to keep an outward focus in our lives, just like Jesus.

> *Do not be anxious about anything, but in everything, by prayer and petition, with thanksgiving, present your requests to God. And the peace of God, which transcends all understanding, will guard your hearts and your minds in Christ Jesus* (Philippians 4:6-7).

Scriptures: Deuteronomy 31:6; Psalm 18, 23, 27:1-3, 34:1-5, 19, 37, 42:5, 56:3-4, 91; Proverbs 3:5-6, 23-24; Isaiah 26:3, 41:10, 41:13, 43:1; Matthew 6:25-34, 10:28; Luke 14:27; John 14:27, 15:1-8, 16:33; Romans 8:28, 15:13; 2 Corinthians 10:5,12:9; Hebrews 13:5b; Philippians 4:4-13, 4:19; Colossians 3:16-17; 1 Timothy 6:6-8; 2 Timothy 1:7; 1 Peter 5:7; 1 John 4:18-19.

9. Fighting Sin by the Power of the Holy Spirit

> *For if you live according to the sinful nature, you will die; but if by the Spirit you put to death the misdeeds of the body, you will live* (Romans 8:13).

You are not in this alone; you have the Holy Spirit's help. A very important key to remember is to ask the Holy Spirit to help you fight against sin and overcome it. Overcome sin by the power of the Holy Spirit. Don't try to come against sin in your own strength. You will need the Holy Spirit's help. We all do!

If you love me you will obey what I command. And I will ask the Father, and He will give you another Counselor to be with you forever-the Spirit of truth. The world cannot accept him, because it neither sees him nor knows him. But you know him, for he lives with you and will be in you (John 14:15-17).

From the moment you put your faith in Jesus, experiencing spiritual birth, you have the Holy Spirit living within you. He is one of the three persons of the Trinity: God the Father, God the Son—Jesus, and God the Holy Spirit. The Holy Spirit will lead, guide, direct, and help us, convict us of sin, warn and counsel us, intercede for us, comfort us, and strengthen, equip, and empower us.

The meaning of redemption is *ransom by the payment of a price.* Jesus paid a high price to redeem you. You are saved out of a state of sin. Do not return to it. Do not live according to your sinful nature. Do not take the cross or the shed blood of Jesus lightly. That is what you are doing if you return to your sin (Hebrews 10:26-31, 1 Peter 1:18-19).

Many times, we see sin and say that the person is really struggling. I think it is not just a sin issue but a love issue. If you really love Jesus with all of your heart, soul, mind, and strength (Mark 12:29-30), would you be participating in that sin if He really came first in your life, and your desire is to please Him?

A few years ago, as I was counseling Emma, I felt compelled by the Holy Spirit to give her a warning as we met for the final session. I told her that she needed to be careful who her friends were, and who she was spending time with (James 4:4 and 1 Corinthians 15:33). I felt the enemy was going to come against her faith in this area. Sure enough, she gradually stopped coming to church. This was a telling sign that she was turning more to the world instead of to the Lord.

Those who live according to the sinful nature have their minds set on what that nature desires; but those who live in accordance with the Spirit have their minds set on what the Spirit desires. The mind of sinful man is death, but the mind controlled by the Spirit is life and peace (Romans 8:5-6).

After Emma had been gone a few months, she returned to church, called me, and wanted to meet. When we met, she proceeded to tell me how she had turned her back on the Lord and was living an immoral lifestyle. I asked her, "Did this involve other people drawing you back into that life of sin?" When she answered yes, I asked her, "Why didn't you heed the warning I gave you? Was I a bad counselor, or did you not listen to the Holy Spirit?" The Holy Spirit will always warn us when we get into a compromising situation. She answered, "I ignored the Holy Spirit."

Emma's story is an example of ignoring the Holy Spirit's help—an unwillingness to put to death the misdeeds of the body, and an unwillingness to listen to and obey the Holy Spirit.

If anyone fails in their spiritual life, it is not because God's grace wasn't sufficient enough, because it is (2 Corinthians 12:9); or because you could not withstand temptation, because you can (1 Corinthians 10:13). It is because of your own failure to remain in an abiding relationship with Jesus.

If Emma had listened to and heeded the Holy Spirit's warning, she would not have given in to sin. Remember to fight sin by asking the Holy Spirit to help you, and He will.

Scriptures: Romans chapter 8, especially 8:4-17, 5:3-5, 15:13; John 14:15-17, 15:1-8, 26, 16:7-11; Hebrews 10:26-31; Acts 2:33, 2:38-39, 9:31; 1 Timothy 4:12; Jude 20; James 4:4; 2 Corinthians 12:9; Galatians 5:16-17; Acts 1:4-8; Ephesians 1:13-14, 5:18; 1 Corinthians 3:16, 6:19-20, 10:13, 12:7-11, 15:33; 1 Peter 1:18-19; Matthew 20:28.

and **WHAT** *Lord* require of you?
DOES THE

To act **JUSTLY** and

To love **MERCY** and

To walk **HUMBLY**
with your *God*

MICAH 6:8

10. What Does the Lord Require of You?

He has told you, O man, what is good; And what does the Lord require of you? But to do justice, to love kindness, and to walk humbly with your God (Micah 6:8 NASB).

The Lord requires us to **do justice**—to do what is right, to be fair. The Lord requires us to **love kindness**—to be kind, to love mercy and to treat others with love and respect. And the Lord requires us to **walk humbly** with our God—being humble, not having pride, always giving God the glory, not exalting yourself. To be just, love kindness, and to walk humbly with Him is what the Lord requires of us.

Many times I have had a person admit to me that they have a hard time reading and understanding the Bible, or that they don't read it at all! It is no wonder they are struggling. They are suffering from spiritual malnourishment. They are not understanding that going to church once a week does not qualify for feeding their spirit. This is often a result of laziness for they are too lazy to read the Word. Proverbs has a lot to say about laziness and being slothful. What it comes down to is this, you will not be able to overcome sin with scripture if you are too lazy to read it!

We are like babies when we first begin our relationship with the Lord. Someone needs to feed us, milk, not solid food. We don't know the Bible, what scripture says, or where to find specific verses in the Bible. Someone needs to come alongside us and help to feed us, giving us spiritual nourishment. Soon we start growing, like a toddler. We can feed ourselves sometimes, but it is messy! We are still needing some help as we move on to solid food. Then, as we grow and mature in the Lord, we can read the Bible, understand it, and apply it to our lives (Hebrews 5:11-14 and Hebrews 6:1-3).

The Key to Overcoming Sin with Scripture

As we submit ourselves to God and His Word by obeying it, reading it, and applying it to our lives, we become a doer of the Word. With the power that is in us by the Holy Spirit, we overcome by the Word of God, the blood of Jesus, and our testimony (Revelation 12:11), and live a life of overcoming sin with scripture.

Teach me your way, Lord, that I may rely on your faithfulness, give me an undivided heart, that I may fear your name (Psalm 86:11).

---

[1] Keith Carroll, *The Christ Culture*

[2] Zondervan's *Life in the Spirit Study Bible footnote*

Be transformed by the RENEWING of your MIND.

⁀10⁀

RENEWING YOUR MIND

Therefore, I urge you, brothers, in view of God's mercy, to offer your bodies as living sacrifices, holy and pleasing to God-this is your spiritual act of worship. Do not conform any longer to the pattern of this world, but be transformed by the renewing of your mind. Then you will be able to test and approve what God's will is-His good, pleasing and perfect will (Romans 12:1-2).

In counseling, we have a Golden Rule: "You cannot want their healing more than they want it," which means a counselor cannot want your healing more than you want it. You have to be willing to do the work! If you want to be healed and set free from your past, the Lord wants to heal you, and He will!

Then comes the work. Closing open spiritual doors in your life is part of that work and essential for living a free and overcoming life. But you must also renew your mind so you can live according to the Word of God and retrain your brain. Walking out your healing is critical to preventing your flesh from acting in accordance with old habits. If you don't learn how to walk out your healing, you will not be able to maintain it.

Three essential steps to maintain your healing

1. **Renewing Your Mind** – Romans 12:1-2. Renewing involves a continual action. You renew your mind by reading, thinking about,

listening to, and memorizing the Word of God, the Bible. It is impossible to renew your mind without reading the Word.

2. Retraining Your Brain

Train yourself to be godly. For physical training is of some value but godliness has value for all things, holding promise for both the present life and the life to come (1 Timothy 4:7-8).

Your mind and your flesh will still want to behave in the old sinful patterns. Why? Because these sinful habits/thoughts have become patterns in your life. Retrain your brain with new habits that bear godly fruit in your life.

3. Walking It Out

Let us fix our eyes on Jesus, the author and perfecter of our faith, who for the joy set before Him endured the Cross, scorning its shame, and sat down at the right hand of the throne of God (Hebrews 12:2).

The Christian life involves walking with the Lord. That means following Him, keeping your eyes on Jesus; truly making Him Lord of your life, and having a close, personal relationship with Him.

Do Not Conform to the Pattern of this World

Do not conform any longer to the pattern of this world, but be transformed by the renewing of your mind (Romans 12:2).

Let's look at what the first part of this verse means, by not conforming to the pattern of this world. We must understand that this current world system is under Satan's rule and thus, is hostile towards God and His people. This world system is built on humanistic wisdom and values. We, as believers, must firmly resist the pressure to conform to it. Forms of worldliness are all around us:

self-centered living, greed, impurity, lust, bad language, ungodly entertainment, sexual immorality, immodest clothing and behaviors, drugs, partying, intoxication, the occult, envy, hatred, etc.

Remember, James 4:4 says: *Friendship with the world is hatred towards God.* A good question to ask yourself is: Does my life look more like the Lord or the world? Worldly thinking says that if it feels good, you should do it, not caring if it hurts others. In the end, it hurts you.

Do not love the world or anything in the world. If anyone loves the world, the love of the Father is not in him. For everything in the world-the cravings of sinful man, the lust of his eyes and the boasting of what he has and does-comes not from the Father but from the world. The world and its desires pass away, but the man who does the will of God lives forever (1 John 2:15-17).

In today's world, our minds are constantly bombarded with thoughts, images, speech, and songs that are contrary to God and His Word. The opposite of conforming to the world's values and ideals is to be transformed by the power and grace of God, and His Word so that our lives and desires line up with His. We do this by renewing our minds.

Renewing Your Mind

Now, let's look at what the second part of Romans 12:2 means when it says, ...*but be transformed by the renewing of your mind.* Renewing your mind is the process by which your thoughts and your will become more and more Christlike. Salvation is the first step. A committed life of obedience to God's Word, by reading and obeying it, will ensure that your mind will be continually renewed to increasing Christlikeness. Reading the Word of God is one of the most important things you can do. It is an essential key to maintaining your healing, being free, and living an overcoming life.

How to Renew Your Mind

1. **Read** the Word of God. Read the Bible daily (Psalm 119:11, 2 Timothy 3:16-17).
2. **Hear** the Word of God. Listen to preaching and teaching of the Word of God (Romans 10:17).
3. **Study** the Word of God. Do in-depth Bible studies, either by yourself or in a group (2 Timothy 2:15, Deuteronomy 6:5-7).
4. **Memorize** the Word of God. Continually be memorizing Scripture. Put verses on index cards and commit them to memory (Psalm 119:11).
5. **Think** about the Word of God. Think about how you can personally apply God's Word to your life (Psalm 1:2, Joshua 1:8, Psalm 48:9).

Notice the common denominator here is the Word of God, the Bible. It is impossible to renew your mind without the Word of God! So many people want to skip this part of their Christian life. Not a good idea. "I don't have enough time to read the Bible," they say. I have even heard, "The only time I read the Bible is in church on Sunday!" This shows where your priorities are.

If you are not willing to renew your mind by reading the Word of God, there will be no growth in your spiritual life. No growth equals a lukewarm life which leads to compromise. As a Christian, one of the most dangerous things you can do is to stop reading the Word.

When we read, hear, study, memorize, and think on the Word of God, it allows the Word to dwell richly in us.

Let the Word of Christ dwell in you richly as you teach and admonish one another with all wisdom, and as you sing psalms, hymns and spiritual songs with gratitude in your hearts to God (Colossians 3:16).

Memorize Scripture

Memorizing scripture is a very important part of renewing your mind. I also talk in chapter 9 about scripture memorization being an important part of learning to overcome sin. I think many times adults think memorizing scripture is just for children's church classes, but I strongly disagree. Scripture memorization brings healing to your mind by renewing it.

> *All Scripture is God breathed and is useful for teaching, rebuking, correcting and training in righteousness, so that the man (or woman) of God may be thoroughly equipped for every good work* (2 Timothy 3:16-17).

> *I have hidden your Word in my heart that I might not sin against you* (Psalm 119:11).

You cannot hide God's Word in your heart by simply reading it once. We are told to be able to give a reason for our faith.

> *But in your hearts set apart Christ as Lord. Always be prepared to give an answer to everyone who asks you to give the reason for the hope that you have. But do this with gentleness and respect* (1 Peter 3:15).

How can we do that without knowing the Word?

Steps to Memorizing Scripture

1. Write the scripture out on an index card. Include the verse and reference, where it is found. Such as:

    > *For God so loved the world, that He gave His only begotten Son, that whosoever believeth in Him should not perish, but have everlasting life* (John 3:16 KJV).

    Carry the card with you and pull it out many times during the day to read and recite it.

2. Say the verse aloud so that you can hear it as well as see it.
3. Think about the verse. I always ask my counselees to tell me what the verse means to them.
4. If it is a long verse, break it down, memorize one phrase at a time, and add each phrase in order until you have the whole verse memorized.

These steps will help you to memorize scripture. After you have the scripture memorized, review it often so it goes into your long-term memory. Over and over again, I have found that memorizing scripture is critical to renewing your mind.

You may feel overwhelmed by the thought of having to renew your mind. I want to encourage you that the Lord is your friend. He will come alongside to help you, and with the Holy Spirit's help, you will be able to renew your mind.

If you feel discouraged or overwhelmed, please remember that He has good plans for your life, plans to prosper you, to give you hope, and a future (Jeremiah 29:11-13). You can succeed in what can seem, at times, as overwhelming circumstances. This is part of the process of sanctification. The Lord is on your side. He will come alongside to help you change and overcome the enemy.

After completing counseling, Annie told me that what helped her so much throughout the process was that I encouraged her that she was not in this alone. I reminded her that the Lord would bless every effort she would make towards Him, even if she felt incapable. She just needed to show up and be willing. He would bless that effort and do the rest.

Scriptures to Encourage You

For I know the plans I have for you, declares the Lord, plans to prosper you and not to harm you, plans to give you hope and a future. Then you will call upon me and come and pray to me, and I will listen to you. You will seek me and find me when you seek me with all your heart (Jeremiah 29:11-13).

Trust in the Lord with all your heart and lean not on your own understanding; in all your ways acknowledge Him, and He will make your paths straight (Proverbs 3:5-6).

For it is by grace you have been saved, through faith-and this not from yourselves, it is the gift of God-not by works, so that no one can boast. For we are God's workmanship, created in Christ Jesus to do good works, which God prepared in advance for us to do (Ephesians 2:8-10).

Come to me, all you who are weary and burdened and I will give you rest. Take my yoke upon you and learn from me, for I am gentle and humble in heart, and you will find rest for your souls. For my yoke is easy and my burden is light (Matthew 11:28-30).

Jesus said to them all, "If anyone would come after me, he must deny himself and take up his cross daily and follow me. For whoever wants to save his life will lose it, but whoever loses his life for me will save it" (Luke 9:23-24).

I have been crucified with Christ and I no longer live, but Christ lives in me. The life I live in the body, I live by faith in the Son of God, who loved me and gave himself for me (Galatians 2:20).

Rejoice in the Lord always. I will say it again: Rejoice! Let your gentleness be evident to all . The Lord is near. Do not be anxious about anything, but in everything, by prayer and petition, with thanksgiving, present your requests to God. And the peace of God, which transcends all understanding, will guard your hearts and minds in Christ Jesus. Finally, brothers, whatever is true, whatever is noble, whatever is right, whatever is pure, whatever is lovely, whatever is admirable-if anything is excellent or praiseworthy-think on these things (Philippians 4: 4-8).

I can do all things through Him who gives me strength (Philippians 4:13).

Peace I leave with you; my peace I give you. I do not give to you as the world gives. Do not let your hearts be troubled and do not be afraid (John 14:27).

Above all else, guard your heart for it is the wellspring of life (Proverbs 4:23).

Finally, all of you, live in harmony with one another; be sympathetic, love as brothers, be compassionate and humble. Do not repay evil with evil or insult with insult, but with blessing, because to this you were called so that you may inherit a blessing (1 Peter 3:8-9).

May the God of hope fill you with all joy and peace as you trust in Him, so that you may overflow with hope by the power of the Holy Spirit (Romans 15:13).

Being confident of this, that He who began a good work in you will carry it on to completion until the day of Christ Jesus (Philippians 1:6).

The Lord is my shepherd; I shall not want. He maketh me to lie down in green pastures: he leadeth me beside the still waters. He restoreth my soul: he leadeth me in the paths of righteousness for his name's sake. Yea, though I walk through the valley of the shadow of death, I will fear no evil: for thou art with me; thy rod and thy staff they comfort me. Thou preparest a table before me in the presence of mine enemies: thou anointest my head with oil; my cup runneth over. Surely goodness and mercy will follow me all the days of my life: and I will dwell in the house of the Lord forever (Psalm 23 KJV).

Additional Scriptures on Renewing your Mind: Deuteronomy 6:5-7; Joshua 1:8; Psalm 1:2, 16:8, 24, 37, 48:9, 51, 91, 103, 119, 121; Proverbs 6:16-19; Jeremiah 29:11-13; Matthew chapters 5,6,7, 6:33, 18:21-35; John 3:16, 14:1-4, 14:27; Romans chapter 8, Romans 8:28-29, Romans 12:1-2; 12:9-12; 2 Corinthians 5:17, 10:5; Galatians chapters 5 and 6; Ephesians chapters 4,5,6; Colossians chapter 3:1-17; 2 Timothy 2:15, 3:16-17; Hebrews 12:1-2,13:5b; James 4:4; 1 Peter 3:15; 1 John 2:15-17.

The consistent renewing of your mind is an integral part of your spiritual growth. The renewal of your mind is demonstrated by an increasingly faithful and obedient response to God's Word. As you purpose in your heart to obey scripture, hide it in your heart, and apply it to your life, your mind will be renewed!

Therefore, if anyone is in Christ, that is grafted in, joined to Him by faith in Him as Savior, he is a new creature, reborn and renewed by the Holy Spirit; the old things, the previous moral and spiritual condition, have passed away. Behold, new things have come, because spiritual awakening brings a new life (2 Corinthians 5:17 AMP).

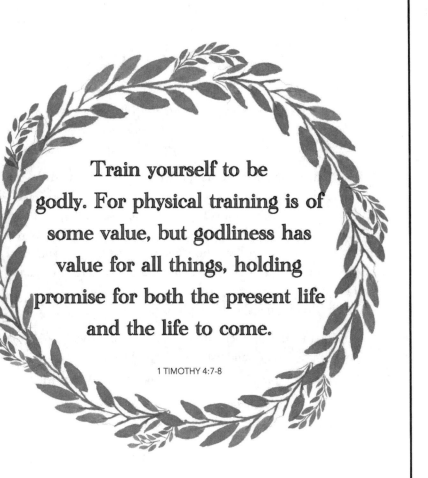

Train yourself to be godly. For physical training is of some value, but godliness has value for all things, holding promise for both the present life and the life to come.

1 TIMOTHY 4:7-8

⤍11⤌

RETRAINING YOUR BRAIN

Train yourself to be godly. For physical training is of some value but godliness has value for all things, holding promise for both the present life and the life to come (1 Timothy 4:7-8).

Sometimes I counsel someone who doesn't want to do the work. They just want God to wave a wand over them and "poof," suddenly they are transformed, renewed, and sanctified, without applying themselves. It does not work that way! In this chapter you will learn the process of how the Bible instructs us to change and what you can do to retrain your brain and get rid of sinful habits and thoughts.

Biblical counseling should help you to:

1. Understand the problem from God's point of view. Ask the Lord to help you to understand your problem.

2. Allow the Lord to give you biblical hope from His Word.

3. Introduce biblical change into your life.

4. Incorporate biblical practice into your life.

Retraining your brain is a very important part of walking out your healing so that you can live an overcoming life. One thing I tell every person I counsel is that this aspect of overcoming takes work! It is just like being in army boot camp. Retraining your brain will be an intense part of their counseling, a part that cannot be skipped. In all of the years of following their own sinful nature and not the Lord, people I counsel have developed habits that are not of God. Since they have closed the doors once opened to the enemy, now they must train their flesh not to behave in those old ways and habits. I call this retraining your brain. It takes time to establish new, godly habits. But once they have done the work, they will have developed good habits and be on their way to retraining their brain. You can use these techniques to retrain your brain too!

So, let's get to work! God shows us in His Word, the Bible, what to do. This is called the biblical structure for change. Remember, the Word of God never says if you feel like it, do it. It says: Do this. Don't do that! God has a specific formula or prescription in His Word. They are what I like to call the "put-offs" and the "put-ons."

Biblical change is initiated in your life through the regenerating power of the Holy Spirit. As a new creation in Christ, you are empowered to make biblical changes in your thoughts, words, and actions (TWAs) as you die to self and desire to do what pleases the Lord rather than your flesh. As you stop or put-off your old continuing pattern of sin and begin to put-on the practice of righteousness and holiness, you are renewed in the spirit of your mind. In order to change your thoughts, words and actions while following the Lord, you must learn and obey God's Word.[1]

I have hidden your Word in my heart that I might not sin against you (Psalm 119:11).

You were taught, with regard to your former way of life to put off your old self, which is being corrupted by its deceitful desires; to be made new in the attitude of your minds; and to put on the new self, created to be like God in true righteousness and holiness (Ephesians 4:22-24).

The Put-Offs and Put-Ons

The Put-Offs: In order to put off the old sinful habits, you must first identify them by examining/judging your life in light of God's Word. (Matthew 7:1-5, 1 Corinthians 11:28-31, 2 Timothy 3:16-17, Hebrews 4:12). Once the sins in your life have been identified, you must repent of them (Proverbs 28:13, 2 Corinthians 7:9-10, Revelation 2:5), confess them (1 John 1:9), and immediately put them aside (Romans 6:12-13a, 2 Corinthians 10:5, Ephesians 4:25, 29, 31, Ephesians 5:4, Colossians 3:1-17, 2 Timothy 2:22a).[2]

The Put-Ons: As you put on righteous deeds (2 Timothy 2:22b, Titus 2:11-12) in the power of the Holy Spirit (Galatians 5:16, Ephesians 3:16-21, 5:18) you will glorify God (1Corinthians 10:31, 1 Peter 4:11), demonstrate your love for Him (Deuteronomy 10:12, Matthew 22:37, 1 John 5:3, 2 John 1:6), and please Him in all things (2 Corinthians 5:9, Colossians 1:10).[3]

It is helpful to pray and ask the Lord what you need to remove (put off) from your life. What behaviors or habits that are not of God? Desiring to please the Lord by putting off thoughts, words and actions that dishonor the name of Christ. And in their place putting on new ways of thinking, speaking, and acting (put on) that reflect the character of Christ.

For example, the Bible says in Ephesians 4:25 to (put off) falsehood and to speak truthfully (put on), to his neighbor, for we are all members of one body.

> *He who has been stealing* [put off] *must steal no longer, but must work, doing something useful with his own hands, that he may have something to share with those in need* [put on] (Ephesians 4:28).

> *Do not let any unwholesome talk come out of your mouths,* [put off] *but only what is helpful for building others up according to*

their needs, that it may benefit those who listen [put on] (Ephesians 4:29).

Get rid [put off] *of all bitterness, rage and anger, brawling and slander, along with every form of malice. Be kind and compassionate to one another, forgiving each other,* [put on] *just as in Christ God forgave you* (Ephesians 4:31-32).

Do not get drunk with wine, which leads to debauchery [put off]. *Instead be filled with the Spirit* [put on]. *Speak to one another with psalms, hymns and spiritual songs. Sing and make music in your heart to the Lord, always giving thanks to God the Father for everything* (Ephesians 5:18-20).

Note: definition of debauchery: sensuality; following one's passions and desires to the point of having no shame or public decency. The words "be filled" carry the meaning in the Greek of repeatedly being filled. We must experience constant renewal by repeatedly being filled with the Holy Spirit.

The acts of the sinful nature are obvious: sexual immorality, impurity, and debauchery; idolatry and witchcraft; hatred, discord, jealousy, fits of rage, selfish ambition, dissentions, factions and envy; drunkenness, orgies, and the like [put off]. *I warn you, as I did before, that those who live like this will not inherit the kingdom of God. But the fruit of the Spirit is love, joy, peace, patience, kindness, goodness, faithfulness, gentleness and self-control* [put on]. *Against such things there is no law. Those who belong to Christ Jesus have crucified the sinful nature with its passions and desires* (Galatians 5:19-24).

Colossians 3:5-14 says: **Put off**—Sexual immorality, impurity, lust, evil desires and greed (which is idolatry), anger, rage, malice, slander, filthy language, and lying. And **Put on**—Compassion, kindness, humility, gentleness, patience, forgiveness, and love.

Memorizing scripture is a great help in implementing the put-off/put-on principle in your life. For example, if you have a problem with swearing or negative talk, you would memorize the following:

> *Do not let any unwholesome talk come out of your mouths, but only what is helpful for building others up according to their needs, so that may benefit those who listen* (Ephesians 4:29).

It is also helpful to ask the Holy Spirit to put a guard on your mouth, so that you do not say anything that is ungodly (see Psalm 141:3). Another important use of scripture is to allow Philippians 4:8 to be a guide for your thought life:

> *Finally, brothers, whatever is true, whatever is noble, whatever is right, whatever is pure, whatever is lovely, whatever is admirable—if anything is excellent or praiseworthy—think about such things.*

If what you are thinking about does not line up with the list above, you don't get to think about it! Lastly, remember to take captive every thought and make it obedient to Christ:

> *We demolish arguments and every pretension that sets itself up against the knowledge of God, and we take captive every thought to make it obedient to Christ* (2 Corinthian 10:5).

This means immediately rebuke the bad thought. Do not think on it, but instead pray and replace the thought with one from Philippians 4:8: Whatever is true, noble, right, pure, lovely, admirable, excellent or praiseworthy, or a psalm, a scripture, or worship song.

Remember, Jesus always had an outward focus in His life. We should too! He was always concerned about others, placing the welfare of others before Himself. Many times, I have found that depression stems from an inward self-absorbed focus. Retrain your brain to think in a Christ-like godly way (Romans 15:1-3, Philippians 2:3-8, Matthew 20:25-28).

Principles to Overcome Bad Habits

Bad habits cover a wide range of negative behaviors. They can be defined as anything that inhibits Christian growth. We may be speaking of sins of the heart such as envy, jealousy, gossip, lying, selfishness, laziness, impatience, quarreling, or procrastination. We may be speaking of various compulsive behaviors such as drinking, smoking, overeating, overspending, gambling, looking at pornography, fantasizing, evil thoughts, masturbation, or swearing.

How Do We Know These Are Bad Habits?

1. **By the Word of God.** Anything that goes against what the Bible says.
2. **By the conviction of the Holy Spirit.** So important to listen and heed what the Holy Spirit is telling you. The Holy Spirit will never contradict what the Bible says.
3. **By WWJD** – What would Jesus do? If Jesus would not do that, we shouldn't either.

What to Do

1. **Repent:** Confess your sins and tell the Lord you are sorry (Proverbs 28:13, Psalm 51).
2. **Pray:** Ask the Lord to forgive you and cleanse you (1 John 1:8-9).
3. **Renew:** Renew your mind daily by reading, hearing, thinking about, studying, and memorizing scripture (Romans 12:1-2).
4. **Purpose:** Determine in your heart and mind to avoid those things that are bad for you and cause you to sin—friends, TV, movies, alcohol, drugs, immorality, etc. (Luke 9:23-24, 1 Corinthians 15:33, 1 John 2:15-17, James 4:4-10, 2 Timothy 2:22, James 4:7-8, Philippians 4:13).

Do not be deceived; God cannot be mocked. A man reaps what he sows. The one who sows to please his sinful nature, from that nature will reap destruction; the one who sows to please the Spirit, from the Spirit will reap eternal life (Galatians 6:7-8).

It is important to remember that bad habits are displeasing to God, and they will certainly lead you into living a life of compromise. We are to walk in newness of life according to Romans 6:1-4. With the Lord's help, we can break these bad habits and form new godly ones.

Remember as you constantly and consistently put off unbiblical thoughts, words, and actions (TWAs), and put on your new thoughts, words, and actions based in the Word of God, you will succeed in having your mind renewed, your brain retrained, and will walk in the newness of Christ.

Scriptures: Deuteronomy 10:12; Proverbs 28:13; Psalm 51, 119:11; Matthew 7:1-5, 20:25-28, 22:27; Luke 9:23-24; Romans 6:1-4, 12-13, 12:1-2, 15:1-3; 1 Corinthians 10:31, 11:28-31, 15:33; 2 Corinthians 5:9, 7:9-10, 10:5; Galatians 5:16, 19-24, 6:7-8; Ephesians 3:16-21, 4:22-32, 5:4, 18-20; Philippians 2:3-8, 4:8, 13; Colossians 1:10, 3:1-17; 1 Timothy 4:7-8; 2 Timothy 2:19, 2:22, 3:16-17; Titus 2:11-12; Hebrews 4:12; James 4:4-10; 1 Peter 4:11; 1 John 1:8-9, 2:15-17, 5:3; 2 John 6; Revelation 2:5.

---

[1] *Biblical Counseling Foundation—Self Confrontation, A Manual for In-Depth Biblical Discipleship.*

[2] ibid

[3] ibid

FOUR THINGS TO DO EVERYDAY

Pray

Read the Bible

Worship

Spend Time in
the presence of
the Lord

☙12☙

WALKING IT OUT

We know that we have come to know him if we obey his commands. The man who says, "I know him," but does not do what he commands is a liar, and the truth is not in him. But if anyone obeys his word, God's love is truly made complete in him. This is how we know we are in him: Whoever claims to live in him must walk as Jesus did (1 John 2:3-6).

Your Christian life involves walking with the Lord: following Him, keeping your eyes on Jesus, truly making Him Lord of your life, and having a close, personal relationship with Him. Walking with the Lord takes purpose, consistency, dedication, and a desire to be pleasing to Him, above all else.

You may experience some conflict within yourself as you make choices between good and evil, between doing what you want and what God wants. As you set your mind to please God instead of yourself, that conflict will resolve. As you walk through your Christian life following these principles and loving Him with all of your heart, soul, mind, and strength, you will become an overcomer.

Love the Lord your God with all your heart and with all your soul and with all your mind and with all your strength (Mark 12:30).

I will show you the way to do that through the principles in this chapter.

Four Daily Spiritual Principles

These are four principles that you need to incorporate into your life on a daily basis: prayer, Bible reading, worship and spending time in the presence of the Lord.

1. **Prayer: the necessary link to receiving God's blessings, the fulfillment of His promises, and the power of the Holy Spirit.**

    Be joyful always; pray continually; give thanks in all circumstances, for this is God's will for you in Christ Jesus (1 Thessalonians 5:16-18).

    Start your day with the Lord in prayer. I believe in dedicating your day to the Lord in prayer before you even get out of bed in the morning. Jesus set aside time every day to pray. How much more should we? Throughout the gospels, it talks about Jesus' prayer life: He withdrew to a solitary place to pray; He got up early to pray; He prayed all night; He went to the garden to pray before the cross. Jesus lived a life of prayer.

    Jesus maintained a lifestyle of prayer, and through it, He brought healing, deliverance, and set the captives free. To have spiritual authority in prayer, you have to be connected to the source! Jesus is the source, and He is the one who heals. Being a pure vessel for Him to flow through is a most important aspect of prayer. Psalm 66:18 says: *If I had cherished sin in my heart, the Lord would not have listened.* Being a pure vessel means salvation, healing, and deliverance can be accomplished for the Kingdom and for His glory.

    Jesus taught us how to pray in Matthew 6:9-15. Prayer is talking to God. It is the multi-faceted communication of believers with the Lord. Sometimes you may think you are too busy to pray. I want to encourage you, that your day will go much better by starting it in prayer. The Bible encourages us to devote ourselves to prayer, and to pray without ceasing; this means continual prayer, a conversation with the Lord in our hearts. This naturally happens as our minds and hearts are focused upon the Lord

An important thing to remember is that there is no power behind our prayers if they are not linked to God and His will. The power in prayer comes from the Lord. Jesus prayed specifically and persistently but always in submission to God and in accordance with the will of the Father. A perfect example of this is when Jesus was about to face the agony of the cross in Matthew 26:36-46.

Jesus also taught us to pray in the Lord's Prayer: "Your Kingdom come; Your will be done." Matthew 6:10. Through prayer we discover what His will is, by aligning our hearts with His, and then praying.

Prayer aligns our hearts with God's will.

Other scriptures on prayer: 2 Chronicles 7:14-16; 1 Samuel 1:1-28; Ezekiel 22:30; Psalm 51, 66:18; Matthew 6:5-15, 7: 7-12, 21:21-22, 26:36-44; Mark 11:24; Luke 6:12, 11:5-13, 22:39; John 15:7, 16:24, chapter 17; Romans 12:12; Ephesians 1:15-23, 3:12-21,6:18-19; Philippians 4:6-7, 19; Colossians 1:9-10, 4:2; 1 Timothy 2:1-8; 1 Thessalonians 5:17-18; Hebrews 4:16,10:22; James 5:13, 5:16; 1 John 3:22; Jude 20.

2. **Read the Bible. The Bible is one of the ways that God talks to us. He will never contradict or go against His Word.**

    I have hidden your Word in my heart that I might not sin against you (Psalm 119:11).

I encourage you to read the Word of God daily. Pray and ask the Lord to give you a love for His Word. Ask Him through the Holy Spirit to help you to understand the Bible, as you are reading it, and to apply it to your life. When you read your Bible, you get to know Jesus better. The Bible gives us direction, helps to keep us from sinning, and has the answers to all of life's questions. What other book can you say that about? The Bible helps us to know

Christ, live in Christ, obey Christ, and witness for Christ.

In the beginning was the Word, and the Word was with God, and the Word was God (John 1:1).

Why Should We Read the Bible?

- The Bible is how God speaks to us. John 1:1
- It reveals who He is. 2 Timothy 3:16
- To get to know the Lord, have a personal relationship, and fellowship with Him. John 3:16-17, 1 John 1:1-4.
- It shows God's love for us. 1 John 4:7-21, John 3:16.
- It produces faith. Romans 10:17, Matthew 21:21-22.
- It encourages us to trust the Lord. Proverbs 3:5-6, Psalm 23.
- It keeps us from sinning. Psalm 119:11
- It brings freedom from sin. 1 John 1:9, Psalm 51.
- It judges the thoughts and attitudes of the heart. Hebrews 4:12
- It is our offensive weapon to fight the devil off with, our sword. Ephesians 6:17
- It keeps us from being deceived. 1 Timothy 4:1, 2 Timothy 3:1-5.
- It brings healing. Exodus 15:26, Isaiah 53:1-5, James 5:14-16
- It brings comfort. The book of Psalms.
- It gives us wisdom. The book of Proverbs. James 1:5
- It directs and teaches us. Psalm 119:105, 2 Timothy 3:16-17.
- It protects us. Psalm 91.
- It manifests truth. The truth sets us free. John 8:36.
- It renews our mind. Romans 12:2
- It strengthens and equips us. Ephesians 4:11-16, Ephesians 6:10-20
- It releases us from condemnation. Romans 8:1

- It enables us to give a reason for the faith we profess. 1 Peter 3:15
- It prepares us for what God has called us to do. 2 Timothy 2:15
- It encourages us that God has good plans for us. Jeremiah 29:11

All that and so much more!

> Billy Graham said: "Long ago I decided to accept the Bible by faith. This should not be difficult for anyone to do. Most of us do not understand nuclear fission, but we accept it. I don't understand television, but I accept it. Why is it so easy to accept all these man-made miracles and so difficult to accept the miracles of the Bible?"[1]

It is helpful to use a Bible in a version that you can understand (NLT, ESV, NIV, NASB, NKJV). A study or life application Bible are good tools also. You can use a Bible reading plan (a Bible reading plan is a way to systematically work your way through the Old Testament and the New Testament), and highlight the verses that stand out to you, as you read. Memorizing scripture, studying the Bible, and attending Bible studies will help you to grow in your faith.

> *So faith comes from hearing, and hearing by the Word of Christ* (Romans 10:17 NASB).

Other scriptures on Bible reading are: Deuteronomy 6:1-7; Psalm 19:7-11, Psalm 119, 138:2; Matthew 5:18; John 1:1-5; Acts 2:29-36, 17:6, 20:32; Romans 10:17, Ephesians 6:12, 4:11-16; 1 Thessalonians 2:13; 1 Timothy 4:11-16; 2 Timothy 2:15, 3:15-17; Hebrews 4:12; James 1:5, 1:22; 2 Peter 1:20-21.

3. **Worship. Ascribing to God the honor, glory, and praise that is due Him.**

> *Shout for joy to the Lord, all the earth. Worship the Lord with gladness; come before Him with joyful songs. Know that the*

Lord is God. It is He who made us, and we are His people, the sheep of His pasture. Enter His gates with thanksgiving and His courts with praise; give thanks to Him and praise His name. For the Lord is good and His love endures forever; His faithfulness continues through all generations (Psalm 100).

Worship is so much more than singing a song about God. The word "worship" is derived from an old English word "worthship" and constitutes those actions and attitudes that ascribe honor and worth to the great God of heaven and earth. Worship is not human-centered but rather God-centered because worship focuses our attention on the Lord rather than on ourselves.

In Christian worship we draw near to God with joy and gratitude for what He has done for us in Christ and through the Holy Spirit. Worship expresses faith, love, and devotion from our hearts and with our lives to God the Father and to the worthy Lamb who was slain for our sins. Worship may express itself in the form of direct address, as in adoration or praise, thanksgiving, singing, or in service to God. It may be done in private or public.[2]

When I am worshipping the Lord, I like to imagine that I am standing before the Lord in the throne room of God. How would I act? How would I give Him glory? I would praise Him with my mouth, raise my hands to Him, or sing a worship song to Him from my heart. My eyes are upon Him and Him alone, with my spirit and soul acknowledging that He is worthy to be praised! Make it a priority to daily worship Him.

Great is the Lord and most worthy of praise; His greatness no one can fathom (Psalm 145:3).

Other scriptures on worship: 1 Chronicles 16:25; Nehemiah 8:5-6; Psalm 18:3, Psalm 29:1-2, Psalm 33:1-3, Psalm 34:1-3, Psalm 48:1-14, Psalm 95:1-7, Psalm 96:4, Psalm 99:5,9, Psalm 100, Psalm 121:1, Psalm 145:3, Psalm 149, Psalm 150; John 4:1-26; Ephesians 5:19-20.

be still *and* know

Psalm 46:10

4. Spend Time in the Presence of the Lord

Be still, and know that I am God; I will be exalted among the nations, I will be exalted in the earth (Psalm 46:10).

Daily spend time in the presence of the Lord, listening, not petitioning during this time. Being content to be in His presence. The Hebrew meaning of this phrase, "be still," can be translated "let go." It means to quit holding on to things that keep you from exalting God and giving Him the proper place of honor in your life. It means spending time with the Lord in His presence without petitioning, doing personal devotions, or Bible study during this time. And it means sitting, being still, listening, and enjoying His presence and fellowship.

It is important that there are no distractions during this time, such as: cell phones, texting, computers, email, Facebook, television, radio, or even music. If you are always busy, never being still, and constantly distracted, you will never spend the time with the Lord or get to know Him, hear His voice, or be in His presence.

He makes me lie down in green pastures, He leads me beside still waters, He restores my soul (Psalm 23:2).

Let's look at the life of David when he was a shepherd. He spent a lot of hours in the fields, watching over the sheep. While doing that, he had time to spend with the Lord: thinking about Him, worshipping Him, and praying. Many Psalms in the Bible were written as a result of David spending that time with the Lord.

Our heavenly Father invites each of us into the fellowship of His presence. To what degree are we listening, observing, and following His lead?[3]

Scriptures that encourage you to spend time in His Presence: Some of these were written by David: Psalm 5, Psalm 23, Psalm 24, Psalm 29, Psalm 30, Psalm 32, Psalm 33, Psalm 34, Psalm 46, Psalm 42, Psalm 37:3-7; John 10:1-18; Acts 4:13.

It is so important to incorporate these four daily spiritual principles into your life. In implementing each one of them—prayer, reading the Bible, worship and spending time in the presence of the Lord—you will find yourself growing and focused on Jesus.

Other Principles to Incorporate Into Your Life

I've stressed how important it is to spend time in the presence of the Lord, read the Bible, worship, and pray. It is also very important for you to have a time where you study the Bible in-depth.

In-Depth Bible Study Time

I will never forget your precepts, for by them you have preserved my life (Psalm 119:93).

Reading the Bible and studying it in-depth, allowing the Lord to speak to you through it and by the Holy Spirit, is crucial to helping you to mature and grow in the Lord.

I encourage you to develop a Bible study plan, such as using a Bible reading plan where you systematically read through the whole Bible, or read and study one book of the New Testament at a time. I believe it is important to read one chapter of Proverbs per day (Proverbs are wisdom for daily living), and you can read one Psalm per day in addition. At our church we have a Bible reading plan called the Spiritual Body Builders (available at Abbasheart.com).

Listen to what the Holy Spirit is encouraging you to add to your faith, then study that. For example: What does the Bible say about the fruit of the Spirit in Galatians 5:22-23? It speaks of love, joy, peace, patience, kindness, goodness, faithfulness, gentleness, and self-control. What does the Bible say about each one? How do we add these attributes to our life? Some wonderful studies I have done are: What does it mean to have a pure heart? How do we guard our hearts? What does it mean to live a blameless life, and how do we do that?

If you don't feel comfortable developing a plan of your own of how to study the Bible, I would encourage you to visit your local Bible bookstore and pick up a Bible reading plan or a written Bible study.

Some use a written, daily devotional guide to get encouragement, but that should not be your only source. To spiritually grow and mature, you must do more than read a devotional each day.

Some like to read the Bible on their phone or computer. I don't encourage that because it is difficult to highlight verses that stand out to you and do in-depth study. Reading the Bible on your phone is fine for your lunch break at work or while you are waiting for an appointment but very difficult to use for in-depth study. This is also due to the fact that with your phone there will be interruptions such as texts, emails, and calls.

Incorporating the practice of reading your Bible in the first part of your day is so important because it starts the day off right and many times you will be too tired by the end of the day.

Jesus read and studied scripture. See Luke 4:14-21 and Luke 2:41-52. As you read and study the Bible in depth, you will develop a love for the Word of God and mature in your faith.

And now I entrust you to God and the message of His grace that is able to build you up and give you an inheritance with all those He has set apart for Himself (Acts 20:32 NLT).

Scriptures: Deuteronomy 6:1-7; Psalm 19:7-11,119; Matthew 4:1-11, 14:23; Luke 2:41-52. 4:14-21, 6:12; John 1:1-2, 10:27-30; Acts 20:32; Romans 10:17; Hebrews 4:12; 1 Thessalonians 2:13; 1 Timothy 4:7-8, 4:11-16; 2 Timothy 2:15, 3:15-17.

Go to Church

First of all, go to a church that honors Jesus Christ and His Word—the Bible—for corporate worship and prayer to receive prayer and encouragement. We also go to church to learn from and gain instruction from the Bible, for Christian fellowship, for evangelism, and for opportunities to serve the Lord!

> *Let us consider how we may spur one another on toward love and good deeds. Let us not give up meeting together, as some are in the habit of doing, but let us encourage one another-and all the more as you see the Day approaching* (Hebrews 10:24-25).

It is so important to meet together regularly in order to encourage and strengthen each other to stand firm in Christ. If we withdraw from the body of Christ and neglect meeting with other believers, we will become weaker, more prone to compromise, and more susceptible to deception and the enemy's schemes.

When someone starts missing church, it is a sign that something is not right with their relationship with the Lord. They are putting other things in place of God. The Bible instructs us in Hebrews 10:24-25 to not give up meeting together. The fourth Commandment says to remember the Sabbath day and keep it holy. That means keeping the day for the Lord by going to church and concentrating on the things of God, and resting.

Billy Graham writes, "The church is primarily the body of Christ...The Bible says that it was Christ's love for the church that caused Him to go to the cross. If Christ loved the church that much...I must love it too. I must pray for it, defend it, work in it, pay my tithes and offerings to it, help to advance it, promote holiness in it, and make it the functional, witnessing body our Lord meant it to be. You go to church with that attitude this Sunday, and nobody will keep you away the next!"[4]

In the New Testament church, worship services consisted of: preaching, reading of scripture, prayer, singing, Baptism, the Lord's Supper (Communion), prophesying and tongues, and worship.

As a Christian, we should look forward to going to church! Going to God's house for worship, prayer, the preaching and reading of the Word of God, Communion, evangelism, and fellowship with other believers, is to be a wonderful, exciting, and best part of our week!

Scriptures: Exodus 20:8-11; Psalm 29:1-2, 48:9, 122:1; Matthew 13:25-30; John 4:23-24; Acts 2:41, 20:7; Romans 12:3-13; 1 Corinthians 12, 13,14, 16:12; Ephesians 4:1-16; Colossians 3:16-17, 4:16; 1 Timothy 4:11-16; Hebrews 10:23-25; James 5:13-16; 1 Peter 2:5, 1 Peter 4:10-11; 1 John 1:7.

Christian Fellowship and Friends

We should have around us only those that will encourage us in our walk with the Lord; those that are sold out to the Lord! These are the friends that you can enjoy true fellowship with. Any person that leads you into sin is not a friend! Don't hang around compromisers! Remember friendship with the world is hatred towards God. It is spiritual adultery (see James 4:4-10).

Bad company corrupts good character (1 Corinthians 15:33).

I remember talking to the Lord about friendship at one time in my life. I said, "Lord, I don't feel like I have any friends." He said to me, "I'm your friend, isn't that enough?" I answered, "Yes, it is." I found the importance of going to the Lord first, instead of running to my friends for answers.

Blessed is the man who does not walk in the counsel of the wicked or stand in the way of sinners or sit in the seat of mockers. But his delight is in the law of the Lord, and on His

141

law, he meditates day and night. He is like a tree planted by streams of water, which yields its fruit in season and whose leaf does not wither. Whatever he does prospers (Psalm 1:1-3).

Scriptures: Psalm 1:1-3; Proverbs 12:26, 17:17, 18:24, 22:11, 22:24, 27:6; 1 Corinthians 15:33; 2 Corinthians 6:14-7:1; James 4:4-10; 1 John 1:7, 2:15-17.

Witnessing

Then Jesus came to them and said: "All Authority in heaven and earth has been given to me. Therefore, go and make disciples of all nations, baptizing them in the name of the Father and of the Son and the Holy Spirit, and teaching them to obey everything I have commanded you. And surely I am with you always to the very end of the age" (Matthew 28:18-20).

This scripture is for all believers. Jesus is telling us to go and make disciples, win the lost, and share the good news of the Gospel. That is why it is called the Great Commission. It is a command He gives that is not just for missionaries, pastors, and evangelists, but for all who follow Christ.

The term "witnessing" is used to describe the process of proclaiming the Christian faith to nonbelievers. As we witness, we tell others of what the Lord has done in our lives, and what we have experienced of God's forgiveness, goodness, mercy, and grace. All Christians are called to witness. We share Christ by our lives, words, and actions. Some unfortunately are bad, ineffective witnesses, living compromised lives. Hopefully this will not be true of us.

We all have a part in bringing in the harvest-witnessing, discipling, baptizing, and teaching. Second Peter 3:9 (NASB) says: *The Lord is not slow about His promise, but is patient towards you, not wishing for any to perish but for all to come to repentance.*

He wants everyone to hear the Gospel. I can tell you that

leading someone to Christ is one of the most exciting things you can do!

Some are reticent to share Christ out of fear of being rejected. This rarely happens. It is a lie the enemy whispers to keep us from sharing the Good News. I find it helpful to pray: "Lord, help me to share the Gospel today. Direct me to the one You want me to minister to and open their heart to receive." You can also pray that their spiritual eyes and ears would be opened. The best witnessing tool you can use is to tell them what the Lord has done for you in your life, what it was like before receiving Christ, and what it is like since you have received Him as Lord and Savior. Tell them of the power Jesus has to transform their lives.

If a person is unsure of their relationship with God, I ask, "If you were to die today, would you go to heaven?" If the answer is "No," or they are uncertain, I ask them, "If you would like to be sure of your relationship with the Lord, would you like to accept Him as Lord and Savior, and have eternal life?" When they answer "Yes," I lead them through the prayer of Faith. (See chapter 1. The prayer for salvation.)

I also find it helpful to carry with me the booklet *Steps to Peace with God* (Billy Graham Evangelistic Association). I hand these out often. It includes an explanation of why we need Jesus, salvation scriptures, and how to accept Him as our Lord and Savior through the prayer of faith.

> *But you shall receive power when the Holy Spirit has come upon you; and you shall be witnesses to Me in Jerusalem, and in all Judea and Samaria, and to the ends of the earth* (Acts 1:8).

Scriptures: Proverbs 11:30; Matthew 4:19, 5:16, 9:35-38, 28:18-20; Mark 16:15; Luke 10:1-2; John 3:16-17; Acts 1:8, 4:13; Romans 1:16, 3:23; 1 Corinthians 9:16, 15:1, 3-4; 2 Corinthians 5:17, 5:19; 1 Timothy 2:4; Philemon 4-7; 1 Peter 3:15; 2 Peter 3:9; 1 John 1:1.

Keeping Your Spiritual and Physical House Clean

It is of utmost importance to take captive every thought and make it obedient to Christ (2 Corinthians 10:5, see chapter 8—Guarding Your Heart). Keeping your mind, body, and spirit pure and accountable to the Lord and His Word is the way to keep your spiritual house clean. Matthew 5:8 says: *Blessed are the pure in heart for they will see God.* Live a life that is pleasing to the Lord.

Along with keeping your spiritual house clean, it is very important to keep your physical home clean also. One time, a friend was co-counseling a woman with me, who had a very disorderly home, like the ones you see on TV shows! She said something I will never forget: "The physical home is a representation of your spiritual house," meaning that if your physical house is a wreck, your spiritual life probably is too.

I tell everyone that I counsel to clean out their homes. This means getting rid of things that have no place in a Christian home such as: immoral books, magazines, movies, pictures, CDs, DVDs, evil games and toys, ungodly music, evil video games, occult and New Age objects, crystals, and religious items such as buddhas, religious icons and artifacts, idols, etc. Many times, objects from foreign countries can come with attachments. Maybe something you inherited should not be in your home or you may have something that is a source of idolatry in your life that you need to get rid of. That is why it is so important to pray as you are cleaning out your house, asking the Lord to direct you.

Let's not forget to clean out your phone, computer, and tablets of bad, immoral or evil apps, websites, pornography, etc.

Pray, and ask the Lord to show you areas of compromise and anything that needs to be removed. Then clean house and throw it all out!

Another time, while counseling a family and helping them to overcome problems that were developing in their household, the Lord showed me that some of the problems were stemming from bad spiritual things the father was bringing home from work. The father worked in a prison. The Lord told me to tell him, to take a "spiritual shower" every day on the way home from work. That made so much sense. You can imagine the oppressive and many times demonic prison environment. So, each day he began to pray on the way home, asking the Lord to cleanse him and remove anything that was not of God, to renew his mind and spirit, taking a spiritual shower.

I believe it is also important to pray over your home. Sometimes problems can stem from someone, maybe a delivery person, neighbor or relative, that has a bad spirit on them, who brought it into your home. Pray and cleanse it out. Ephesians 6:12 says: *For our struggle is not against flesh and blood, but against the rulers, against the authorities, against the powers of this dark world and against the spiritual forces of evil in the heavenly realms.*

Scriptures: Joshua 24:15; Psalm 51, 91, 119:1-3; Proverbs 3:24; Matthew 5:8; 1 Corinthians 10:14; 2 Corinthians 10:5, 6:19; Ephesians 6:10-12; Colossians 3:1-14, 4:2; 1 Thessalonians 4:1-8, 5:17, 5:22-24; James 4:7-10; 1 John 2:15-17, 3:6, 3:9-10, 5:21.

Your Physical Body

Your body is the temple of the Holy Spirit (1 Corinthians 6:19-20). Let's be good to it. The following are seven things I share with every person I teach and counsel:

1. Eat healthy.

2. Drink lots of filtered, pure water.

3. Exercise.

4. Sunshine. Spend at least 10 minutes a day outside getting some sunshine. It provides vitamin D and elevates your mood.

5. Get a hobby. Hobbies are fun and help to relieve stress.

6. Limit or eliminate TV, video games, social media. Aside from being a waste of time, it distracts you from doing what you're supposed to be doing. Don't waste your life!

7. Sleep. Need I say more?

Walking out your Christian life, keeping your eyes upon Jesus, loving Him, spending time in His presence, obeying His Word, picking up your cross daily and following Him, and incorporating these spiritual principles into your life are all essential keys to walking it out and living a free and overcoming life with Him.

---

[1] *The Billy Graham Christian Worker's Handbook*

[2] Zondervan's *Life in the Spirit Study Bible*

[3] Keith Carroll, *The Christ Culture*

[4] *The Billy Graham Christian Worker's Handbook*

I can do ALL THINGS through CHRIST who strengthens Me.

Philippians 4:13

⮐13⮑

BEING AN OVERCOMER

Be an overcomer, rather than letting your circumstances overcome you! It is so important to live our lives as an overcomer in Christ because the Lord wants to be able to use our lives to witness to those around us. If we are constantly overwhelmed by the circumstances of daily life, we are not living as an overcomer! Being an overcomer is an ongoing process.

As we walk out our faith, what do we need to watch out for? How do we keep the enemy from hindering our walk with the Lord? Learn how to hear the voice of the Lord, persevere in your faith, prefer Him, and run your race to make a difference for the Kingdom of God!

The Three Ds: Discouragement, Depression, Distractions

I tell everyone I counsel to watch out as they grow for what I call the 3 Ds! They are: discouragement, depression, and distractions. If the enemy can get us in any of these three areas, he will be successful in hindering our walk with the Lord. We will not be effective for the Kingdom if we are overcome in any of them.

Distractions are, unfortunately, a part of our daily life. When something comes across my path, I always try to ask the Lord whether this is a distraction or something I need to pay attention to. More often than not, it is a distraction with the purpose of keeping me from doing what God intends.

For example, one day while writing this book I was sitting at my desk, and my whole house started to vibrate and shake. Living in California, my first thought was that it was an earthquake. But it didn't feel like an earthquake. I got up and looked at my dining room light fixture. It wasn't moving, but my house was still shaking. I looked out my back door. The land behind my house was being developed, and I saw that there was a huge machine directly behind my fence leveling the ground! The shaking and vibrating continued for the next few hours. I decided that this was a distraction and continued to write!

The other two Ds, discouragement and depression, are usually a result of not enough time spent in the Word of God and being inwardly focused. (I discuss this in chapter 11. I am not talking here about a person who has depression stemming from a chemical imbalance in their brain.) A believer can be depressed because of spiritual disobedience and/or unresolved sin, especially in areas such as anger, jealousy, grudges, bitterness, and immorality. That is why we must immediately deal biblically with the sin in our lives. Depression can also be a result of being overwhelmed by the cares of this world, trying to control things, and not trusting the Lord.

So, keep an eye out for the 3 Ds and fix your eyes on Jesus!

Let us fix our eyes on Jesus, the author and perfecter of our faith, who for the joy set before him endured the Cross, scorning its shame, and sat down at the right hand of the throne of God (Hebrews 12:2).

Being Thankful and Counting Your Blessings

I will bless the Lord at all times; His praise shall continually be in my mouth (Psalm 34:1 ESV).

Counting your blessings puts you in a position of being thankful to the Lord for what He has done in your life and for the many things He has blessed you with, such as salvation, life, and breath. It is certainly a key to being an overcomer that we do not want to forget.

The example that stands out to me most is from my own life. I was a young mom with a four-year-old son, Brent, and a newborn, Gregory. One day, Brent became very sick, running a fever, and we noticed he had hemolyzed blood cells in his urine. Praying, we took him to the children's hospital.

It took the doctors three days to diagnose and start treating the problem. During this time, the doctors were mentioning some very troubling possible diagnoses. All the while, Brent's red blood cell count dropped seriously low. Our newborn, Gregory, couldn't come in to the hospital, and Allen and I would not leave Brent's side.

It was a very traumatic time for Brent (and me) due to the many times they came into his room to draw blood for tests. Being four, he would scream and cry out for me not to let them.

One night during all of this, the Lord brought a song to my mind, "I am the Lord that healeth thee, I spoke the Word and healed your disease,"—a scripture put to music based on the verse out of Exodus 15:26.

> *He said, "If you listen carefully to the voice of the Lord your God and do what is right in his eyes, if you pay attention to his commands and keep all his decrees, I will not bring on you any of the diseases I brought on the Egyptians, for I am the Lord, who heals you."*

At that point, Brent had not been diagnosed with a disease. The next morning, Brent was diagnosed with Combs Positive Hemolytic Anemia, a rare disease in which a virus gets into the bloodstream and attaches itself to the red blood cells. This meant that when Brent's white blood cells came to destroy the virus, they ended up destroying his red blood cells too. This is very dangerous as we need red blood cells to live because they carry oxygen to our lungs. It was a rare blood disease, not hereditary or contagious.

They started treatment, and a few days later we were released to go home. I remember being home with both of the boys and crying out to the Lord, "Lord, I need to hear your voice. Is Brent going to be okay?" I will always remember the Lord saying to me, "I have healed Brent and his blood is pure." This was the first time I ever heard the voice of the Lord. From that point on, his red blood count steadily rose, though he would still have to go through months of more blood tests.

Gregory, in the meantime had stopped eating and would not take a bottle. I was trying my best as a mom to hold everything together, keeping my eyes on Jesus and praying without ceasing, when the unthinkable happened—a rat died in my attic! And it stunk! Bad! This rat was my tipping point!

Thankfully, in walked my pastor's wife, Sister Wood. What a breath of fresh air she was! Of course, she had a story about when a rat died in her attic in Africa! It made me feel that I wasn't alone in my rat distress.

She encouraged me that what I needed to do was to start counting my blessings, giving praise to the Lord, and being thankful to Him in all circumstances. I needed to thank the Lord for everything: my home, my husband and children, my family, and on and on. This put my focus back on the Lord and not on my circumstances. It refocused my attention on what really mattered and took it off of the distractions of life.

Give thanks in all circumstances, for this is God's will for you in Christ Jesus (1 Thessalonians 5:18).

I learned a very valuable lesson: in all things to give thanks, to count my blessings, keeping my eyes on the Lord and not upon my circumstances. I learned He will see me through. He will see you through too.

I have set the Lord always before me; because He is at my right hand, I shall not be shaken (Psalm 16:8 ESV).

At the right hand is a place of honor. It is keeping the Lord in a place of honor in your life, setting Him always before you, keeping your eyes on Him and not on your circumstances. This prevents you from being overwhelmed by your problems and increases your faith as you trust in Him. Counting your blessings and giving thanks to Him in all circumstances, and praising Him (Psalm 150:6) are very important principles and keys to living an overcoming, victorious life with the Lord.

Be joyful in hope, patient in affliction, faithful in prayer (Romans 12:12).

Scriptures: Joshua 1:9; Exodus 15:2,15:26; Psalm 16:8, Psalm 34:1, Psalm 100:4-5, Psalm 121, Psalm 150:6; Romans 12:12; Philippians 4:4-8; Colossians 3:15-17; Hebrews 10:23; 1 Thessalonians 5:16-18.

Hearing the Voice of the Lord

A primary part of prayer is learning to hear the voice of the Lord through the Holy Spirit.

In John 10:27 Jesus said: *My sheep listen to my voice; I know them and they follow me.* This means that all of us, as Christians, have the ability to hear God's voice, but not all of us strive to.

There are three voices you can hear:

1. **The voice of God/The Holy Spirit**—His voice will always line up with the Bible and never contradict it.

2. **The voice of our flesh**—this voice is all about gratifying desires of the sinful nature with selfish things such as: relax, you don't need to read the Bible, skip church, go to the lake, slothfulness, laziness, etc. Say "no" to the voice of the flesh.

3. **The voice of the enemy/Satan**—He is the accuser of the brethren. He comes to accuse, condemn, steal, kill, threaten, lie, and destroy. Rebuke and silence him. Matthew 4:10.

The more you read the Word, the more obedient you become in your walk. The more you remove distractions from your life that keep you from hearing His voice, the more you settle down and spend time in the presence of the Lord, the more you will hear His voice. I have found that as I listen and obey His voice, His voice becomes even clearer.

Scriptures: Psalm 46:10; Matthew 4:1-11, 16:23, Luke 4:1-14; John 8:44, 10:10, 10:1-30; 1 Corinthians 10:13; James 1:13-15, 4:4-8; Rev. 12:10.

When a Breakthrough Is Not Happening

Sometimes a breakthrough can stall. If this happens to you, I have found these three areas important to check in your life.

1. **Brokenness** – Psalm 51:17: *The sacrifices of God are a broken spirit; a broken and contrite heart O God, you will not despise.* Sometimes a person refuses to let themselves be broken with what breaks God's heart. This usually results from an unwillingness to separate themselves from sin. They have to be willing for the Lord to take them to a place of brokenness before Him.

2. **Submitting your will to God** – Matthew 6:10: *Your Kingdom come Your will be done.* An unwillingness to submit their will to God usually comes from people who are very stubborn. They resist submitting their will to the Lord. James 4:7 instructs us to: *Submit yourselves then, to God. Resist the devil and he will flee.* If this is the case, I encourage them to begin their day by praying: "Lord, I submit my will to Yours." Pray this prayer several times a day if necessary.

3. **Denying yourself** – Jesus said in Luke 9:23-24: *If anyone would come after me, he must deny himself and take up his cross daily and follow me. For whoever wants to save his life will lose it, but who-*

ever loses his life for me will save it. An unwillingness to submit one's will to God is a refusal to die to self. A choice must be made between living for ourselves and our own selfish desires and living for God. This choice must be made and upheld. That choice will determine our eternal destiny.

Add to Your Faith

For this very reason, make every effort to add to your faith goodness; and to goodness, knowledge; and to knowledge, self-control; and to self-control, perseverance; and to perseverance, godliness; and to godliness, brotherly kindness; and to brotherly kindness, love. For if you possess these qualities in increasing measure, they will keep you from being ineffective and unproductive in your knowledge of our Lord Jesus Christ (2 Peter 1:5-8).

It is very important to add these seven qualities to our faith. Godly characteristics do not automatically grow without diligent effort on our part. These qualities will grow in our lives, as we study the Word of God and apply it to our lives. When these qualities are added to our faith, they will keep us from being ineffective and unfruitful in our walk with the Lord. This is a beautiful promise of God!

Preferring the Lord

Preferring the Lord is an action of the attitude of your heart. Preferring Him is an inward sincere desire of your heart. It is putting the Lord first in all that you do. Preferring Him. Jesus said in Mark 12:30 that we are to love the Lord our God with all of our heart, soul, mind, and strength. As we endeavor to do this, we prefer Him.

I often remind those I counsel to prefer the Lord in all of their actions, desires, and decisions. Sometimes I will ask the question:

"Are you preferring the Lord?" Many times, I will see that they are preferring their flesh and not the Lord. They are following after the sinful nature and their flesh. (See Galatians 5:19-21.) Many times we do not understand that our sinful actions hurt the Lord.

Not preferring the Lord can include: being drawn to the things of this world, swearing or using bad language, an impure relationship, anger, unforgiveness, discord, immorality, and so much more. Not preferring Him is when we choose to go against scripture, what the Bible says. Many problems can be avoided if we would just prefer the Lord!

As we purpose in our heart to please the Lord in all we do, we prefer Him. Each day, each hour, and even each minute of our lives we need to choose to prefer Him. What peace and freedom that brings. I choose to prefer the Lord, and I hope you will too.

Perseverance, Persecution, and Running Your Race

Perseverance

Consider it pure joy, my brothers, whenever you face trials of many kinds, because you know that the testing of your faith develops perseverance. Perseverance must finish its work so that you may be mature and complete, not lacking anything (James 1:2-4).

Let's look at the parable of the ten virgins that Jesus told in Matthew 25:1-13. Please read this parable. This parable teaches us, that we, as believers, need to persevere in our faith to be ready for the Lord's return. We all need to have our own supply of oil; the oil in this parable symbolizes a pure heart, true faith, righteous living, and obedience to God's Word and the Holy Spirit.

We must persevere in our faith to purchase our oil, having a good supply of this oil (faith) and not letting anyone take away our oil! Each one had to persevere and earn their own oil, which was earned through a pure faith and obedience to the Lord.

Five were foolish and not prepared for His return. They did not take any oil with them to meet the bridegroom. The other five, took oil with them and trimmed their lamps. The bridegroom was a long time in coming, and they all fell asleep.

We must be prepared and ready for His return. We must persevere in our faith so that when the day and hour arrive, we will be ready to be received by the Lord. Failure to be in a personal relationship with the Lord at the time of His coming will mean you will be excluded from His presence and His Kingdom.

> *Later the others also came, 'Sir! Sir!' they said. 'Open the door for us!' But he replied, 'I tell you the truth, I don't know you.' Therefore keep watch, because you do not know the day or the hour* (Matthew 25:11-13).

Remember, all ten were surprised; five were ready, but five were not.

> *But seek first His kingdom and His righteousness, and all these things will be given to you as well* (Matthew 6:33).

Persecution

> *Jesus said: "Blessed are those who are persecuted because of righteousness, for theirs is the kingdom of Heaven. Blessed are you when people insult you, persecute you and falsely say all kinds of evil against you because of me. Rejoice and be glad, because great is your reward in Heaven"* (Matthew 5:10-12).

Persecution will be the lot of all who seek to live in harmony with God's Word for the sake of righteousness. When you uphold God's standards of truth, justice, and purity in your life and refuse to compromise with the present evil society or the lifestyles of lukewarm believers (Rev. 2, 3:1-4, 14-22), you may experience unpopularity, rejection, and criticism.

Persecution and opposition will come from the world (Matthew 10:22, 24:9, John 15:19), and at times from those within the professing church (Acts 20:28-31, 2 Corinthians 11:3-15, 2 Timothy 1:15, 3:8-14, 4:16). When experiencing this persecution, Christians are to rejoice, for to those who suffer most, God imparts the highest blessing (2 Corinthians 1:5, 2 Timothy 2:12, 1 Peter 1:7, 4:13).[1]

> *These have come so that your faith—of greater worth than gold, which perishes even through refined by fire—may be proved genuine and may result in praise, glory and honor when Jesus Christ is revealed* (1 Peter 1:7).

One time, when I was experiencing some persecution in my Christian walk, a friend encouraged me. She told me that, if everything was going smooth in her own life all of the time, she would think that she must not be doing enough for the Kingdom of God if she wasn't experiencing at least some persecution! Wow! That changed my way of thinking. Too many times we want the Lord to rescue and remove us from all forms of persecution and trouble. Instead, we need to count it all joy!

> *Blessed is the man who perseveres under trial, because when he has stood the test, he will receive the crown of life that God has promised to those who love Him* (James 1:12).

Running Your Race

> *Therefore, since we are surrounded by such a great cloud of witnesses, let us throw off everything that hinders and the sin that so easily entangles, and let us run with perseverance the race marked out for us. Let us fix our eyes on Jesus, the author and perfecter of our faith, who for the joy set before Him endured the cross, scorning its shame, and sat down at the right hand of the throne of God* (Hebrews 12:1-2).

Our race is our lifelong test of faith. We are to run our race with purpose, perseverance, and patience, keeping our eyes on the Lord, and of course, endurance, throwing off all sin that entangles us. We are to fix our eyes on Jesus, trusting Him to help us to complete the race with honor and strength.

We want to stand before the Lord at the Judgment Day and hear, "Well done, good and faithful servant!" Our desire should be as Paul, when he said in 2 Timothy 4:7-8:

> *I have fought the good fight, I have finished the race, I have kept the faith. Now there is in store for me the crown of right-eousness, which the Lord, the righteous Judge, will award to me on that day—and not only to me, but also to all who have longed for His appearing.*

> *Whatever you do, work at it with all your heart, as working for the Lord, not for men, since you know that you will receive an inheritance from the Lord as a reward* (Colossians 3:23-24).

Scriptures: Matthew 5:10-16, 6:33, 10:22, 32, 11:28-30, 24:9, 25:1-13; John 14:1-4, 14:27, 15:19, 16:33; Acts 20:28-31; Romans 5:35, chapter 8, 12:12,14, 9-21; 2 Corinthians 1:5, 5:17, 11:3-15; Galatians 2:20; Philippians 3:7-14, 4:13; Colossians 3:23-24; 2 Timothy 2:22-26, 3:1-5, 3:10-12, 4:7-8; Hebrews 10:23, 10: 19-39; Hebrews chapters 11 and 12; James 1:2-4, 5:7-11, 4:7-10; 2 Timothy 1:15, 2:12, 3:8-14, 4:16; 1 Peter 1:7, 3:8-9, 4:13; Revelation 2, 3:1-4, 14-22.

> *But one thing I do: Forgetting what is behind and straining toward what is ahead, I press on toward the goal to win the prize for which God has called me heavenward in Christ Jesus* (Philippians 3:13-14).

Finally, I would like to end this chapter with a story from one who is successfully walking it out. It is a testimony of the Lord's redemptive power from one who was formerly in bondage and had an open door in the area of drugs:

It was a beautiful warm summer day. There was a refreshing wind blowing as my family and I set out to pick up a used part for one of our cars. As we arrived at the lot, we set out on a scavenger hunt to find the part for our old, faithful little vehicle. Checking the map, we found a row of cars that were the right year, make, and model. The kids were laughing and playing as we wound our way through the maze of cars. Then we found the car. As the kids were at the front of the vehicle, I opened the trunk. I froze, then started to weep silently. In a split second, a million memories raced through my mind. Images of unspeakable horror, tragedy, treachery, indescribable pain, and hopelessness.

It very quickly dissipated into gratitude and peace. My eyes overflowed with silent tears of joy as I realized such redemption the Lord had wrought in my life. A bag of syringes lay open there in the trunk. Decades of drug addiction, and I had forgotten it was ever even a part of my life. How could such complete redemption be possible? Only Calvary could accomplish such a perfect and complete redemption. Jesus and He alone, who paid the price for my sin, could redeem a life so perfectly.

The grip of addiction was nothing compared to the power of His love. A song based on Psalm 103 came to my mind; "As far as the East is from the West, that's how far He has removed our transgressions from us." As I closed the trunk, putting the bag out of sight, no one was even aware of it. I will always be grateful for this perfect moment God afforded me, to realize the depth of His miraculous redemption of my life.

Remaining in Christ

No, despite all these things, overwhelming victory is ours through Christ, who loved us. And I am convinced that

*nothing can ever separate us from God's love. Neither death nor
life, neither angels nor demons, neither our fears for today nor
our worries about tomorrow-not even the powers of hell can
separate us from God's love. No power in the sky above or in the
earth below-indeed, nothing in all creation will ever be able to
separate us from the love of God that is revealed in Christ Jesus
our Lord* (Romans 8:37-39 NLT).

An important part of being an overcomer is purposing in your
heart to never open these doors to the enemy again. How do we do
that? The answer is to remain in Christ.

If anyone fails in their spiritual life, it is not because God's
grace wasn't sufficient enough because it is (2 Corinthians 12:9).
Or because you could not withstand temptation, because you can
(1 Corinthians 10:13). It is because of our own failure to remain in
an abiding relationship with Jesus Christ.

Failing at being an overcomer happens because we neglect to
remain in Christ (see John 15:4-8, Romans 8:37-39, Rev. 21:7). As
we remain in Him, the doors we have closed in our lives will remain closed.

By Remaining in Christ:

1. Remaining in Christ, we are assured of never opening these
   doors to the enemy again.

2. Remaining in Christ, we have the certainty that we will never
   be separated from God's love.

3. Remaining in Christ, we are assured of being an overcomer.

As we remain in Him, we are empowered by the Holy Spirit to
be an overcomer and proclaim the testimony of Jesus to the world.

In writing this book, I have sought to share insight, principles, and keys the Lord has given me. Sharing them with those I counsel and disciple and with you, as well, because the Lord desires for us to walk in His healing and wholeness, being equipped by Him, reaching our full potential, and fulfilling our spiritual destiny.

As you implement the daily spiritual principles and keys into your life and close any open doors, you will be able to be an overcomer and live free. This is so important because the Lord has a job for us all to do. We are called to take part in the harvest and spread the gospel to those who don't know Christ.

Jesus said in John 4:35: *I tell you, open your eyes and look at the fields! They are ripe for harvest.*

As we determine to live each day in a manner that pleases the Lord, preferring Him, we lift Jesus up in our lives, and draw others to Him. We can tell them about what He has done in our lives and the goodness of the Lord. We can tell them about His peace that passes understanding and of His love for them.

> My hope and prayer for you, is that you will close the open doors in your life and apply the keys given in this book to go forth, be free, and live an overcoming life in Jesus, bearing much fruit for the Kingdom.
> Much love in the Lord,
> Caryn
>
> *The Lord is faithful, and He will strengthen you, setting you on a firm foundation, and will protect and guard you from the evil one* (2 Thessalonians 3:3 AMP).

---

[1] *Biblical Counseling Foundation-Self Confrontation, A Manual for In-Depth Biblical Discipleship*

WHATEVER you do
WHETHER IN *word* OR *deed*
DO IT ALL
IN THE NAME
of the *Lord Jesus*
giving thanks to
God **THE**
FATHER
through Him.
Colossians 3:17

∾14∾

TESTIMONIES

"I never imagined the freedom I would receive from closing the four doors to addictions, immorality, the occult, and generational sins. As I closed each door, I felt relief, and the weight lifted off of me. I have yearned for a long time to have the peace I now have since closing those doors.

"I will forever be grateful as my life will never be the same. The ability to take every thought captive has become natural. I no longer allow things that used to bother me, take space in my head. Closing these doors has freed me of guilt, shame, and disappointment with myself for past things. I look forward to seeing the continued change in myself as I put God first in all I do!" —N.P.

———⟫◆⟪———

"Before I closed the doors I had opened in my life, I was bound in my mind. I never had peace, I had no identity, and I was lonely and rejected. I would hear the words of these things all the time in my mind, and I was just a mess. My mind was just so noisy, and it would never shut up. Finally, I was ready to give up the fight. I was really ready.

"As I was going through the four doors to close them, the Lord gave me a vison that I like to call the hallway of doors. While I relinquished my sins over to the Lord and told Satan that I'm cleansed by the blood of Christ and he can no longer have me, I saw the doors being bolted shut from top to bottom. Then the Lord showed me Satan running through the hallway trying to open them back up. Jesus then showed me that he bound Satan up now, and he can no longer get to me. Jesus then proceeded to take me to another door in the hallway. It was the Lord's door. It was huge, wide, and tall. He took me by the right hand, and we went through the door. It was a land of paradise.

"I found myself in complete freedom! It brought joy to my heart, and I knew I was loved. So many lies were exposed, and many more sweet things came from the Lord. I felt every presence of goodness fall over me as I walked through the Lord's door with Him, and my mind was set free. I could literally feel the weight lifted off my shoulders.

"To stay in this paradise, I keep my eyes on Jesus by spending time with Him, reading the Bible, worshiping Him, keeping my heart clean, memorizing scripture, taking my thoughts captive, not listening to ugly things, or watching ugly things. Every time the enemy comes to yell at me and remind me of my past, I remind him the scriptures of God's Word, just like Jesus did in the wilderness.

"And when my flesh tries to rise up, I make it come into the obedience of Christ by the Word of God. You See, I never knew what true peace was until I shut these doors. These doors hindered me from God being able to reveal himself to me, because God doesn't dwell in darkness, He's too good. But once I was set free, I felt the most beautiful peace flow over me and I walk with that peace still today." —P.B.

"Before counseling, I had many doors open. They were left wide open, unattended, simply because I had no idea that by living loosely in my Christian walk would invite the enemy to come in and wreak havoc in my life. Since learning how to close doors and keep them closed, my life has been more peaceful, and my mind is quiet. Closing these doors was the key for me to becoming an overcoming Christian.

"After closing the spiritual doors that had been opened, there was a peace that came over me like I had never experienced. It was the peace of the Lord. I also experienced a quiet mind. Before closing these doors and kicking the enemy out I never knew I needed a quiet mind. I was so accustomed to the chaotic noise, thoughts, and lies the enemy was constantly feeding me that I just thought it was normal. I am so grateful to the Lord for the power He has given us to close these doors and kick out the enemy.

"I remember Caryn teaching me to pray over my home daily and especially if someone comes into my home, like a repair person, or even family. I never realized the importance of this until the first time I forgot to pray over my home after a repair person came in. It affected not only me but my husband and children as well. There was frustration and strife for no reason between us. When we finally figured out it was an attack from the enemy, we quickly took care of it in prayer.

"Another thing that I learned from Caryn was about spiritual attachments in objects. I remember hearing the phrase we need to clean out our physical house as well as spiritual. I was a little confused at first, but with her guidance, I came to understand its importance. During that season of counseling, I physically went through every drawer and cabinet in my home. I found SEVERAL items that needed to be tossed out, things that triggered memories of old habits and worldly living as well as things that I got in other countries, such as jewelry, décor, etc. Those are things that the Lord told me personally to toss out.

"By doing this and by choosing to be careful on what I allow in the home has helped me to be aware of the enemy and not allow him to get even a foothold in my life." —C.S.

⸺⊰◆⊱⸺

"The Lord has helped me to overcome so much shame. Now I know the Lord is the Master at destroying shame. I was practically swimming, no, drowning in shame.

"For me, closing doors in prayer (and not just a thought prayer, but speaking it out loud as a declaration) has had a profound and deep impact on my heart and mind. The doors of sin that I opened in my past held behind them rooms filled with debilitating shame. I didn't talk about what was hidden in these secret rooms to anyone and could fool so many people into thinking I was perfectly happy. I could fool everyone in fact. I could fool everyone, that is, except for one person, Jesus.

"So you can imagine how difficult it was for me to try and pray, knowing He saw every detail of what was inside the 'secret' chambers in my heart. I'd want to pray for a good thing but deep down I knew He was always looking at me with an expression on His face asking, 'When are we going to talk about your secret, shame-filled rooms?'

"I knew I didn't have the strength of character or willpower on my own to say no to going back into these rooms. I know because I tried countless times over many, many years. I didn't want to fail Him again. I was tired of failing.

"However, Jesus helped me to understand something, and it made all the difference. The doors to these rooms were made of the wood of the cross He bore for me. He helped me see the blood stains that the wood was drenched in. He said to me, 'You cannot close these doors in your own strength. You need my strength. I am asking you to do your part only, and I will do the rest. I am only asking you to put your hand on the door.' In my mind I picture myself putting my hand on the door when I pray out loud. He then puts His hand over mine, and we close the door together. He gave me the strength to close that door, and it is kept closed through the blood of Jesus." —G.G.

———❖———

"I had been struggling with many things as a Christian. I really didn't understand why until I had taken a class on closing doors. My birth mother was a drug addict, alcoholic, physical and sexual abuser...a pedophile. I was born into such a mess of an experience, and it had followed me wherever I went. I was adopted at age two and a half, and so my adoptive family never knew what happened, and they were not Christians. This early base of events of physical and spiritual abuse opened doors to the enemy that had affected me my whole life.

My behavior, my mental health, and my identity were all wrapped up in it. I had no idea until the memories surfaced when I turned 40 years old. It broke me. I had two autistic children and a husband to take care of. I pushed through each day, having breakdowns throughout the day when I could spare a moment between crises with the kids. I knew the Lord was there, pulling me through, or I would have ended my life. I had been a Christian for 20 years but went to a church that had never taught on spiritual awareness at all, so I had no idea how to get help. Then, as He does, the Lord showed up! I ran into a friend who went to a church that taught the full spiritual story and could help me.

"I was taught how to close generational doors to the enemy and to close doors on any sexual assaults. I was set free! I no longer have those identity issues or the feelings that used to confuse me. I walk daily with the Lord, in His Word and presence.

"I am so grateful for the peace that He affords me in our families life. The heavy burdens I had carried all my life were cast off, and I could finally breathe. I will never stop being grateful for all the Lord has done and continues to do for me every day. Keeping my mind on Him through the reading of His Word and prayer is how I continue to grow closer to Him. I sit in His peace and presence, even in moments throughout the day, just loving Him and letting Him love me, which can be hard as I walk out my healing. It is a process that He is teaching me to be patient with as He continues to reveal truth to me." —A.B.

"The Lord has done a lot for me within a short period of time. I've always loved the Lord but didn't understand how much past things I had done could affect your walk with Him. I've learned to close open doors to past relationships, habits, and generational issues that were passed down from my parents.

"In my time counseling, I drew closer to the Lord. I learned to depend on Him for my needs and confidence. With scriptures like Philippians 4:13, I learned, 'I can do all things through Christ who strengthens me.' It reminded me daily that no matter what I was going through, God was with me every step of the way.

"In the process, I was also able to change my mindset on a lot of things by prayer and fellowship with the Lord. I asked him to renew my mind and give me strength daily and often quoted Romans 12:2. I am in the process of being renewed and restored through His Word. I continue to pray and trust the Lord. I keep learning to walk closer to God through prayer and scripture. I work on growing as a Christian by remembering all that I learned and putting that into action, as well as never giving up." —T.C.

———◆———

"The Lord has changed how I view things by changing my perception of true faith. If you don't know true faith then you can't function. I had roots of rejection and unforgiveness and a lot of issues with anger from my past. I learned how to close the doors on things from my past that had kept me hindered.

"The first issue that I dealt with was from my childhood. I was bullied from first grade on. Seeing that side of people made me look for only the bad in them. I learned to see people as God's creation, to see them through His eyes, and I learned to truly forgive. Having that root of unforgiveness in my life had left me hindered and angry. The Lord pulled the roots of rejection and unforgiveness out of my life and I was able to truly forgive.

"I learned to walk in healing by taking my personal time with the Lord and renewing my mind with His Word every day. When I lack in any area, it sends me back to square one. Daily prayer, worship, and the Word are the keys to keeping the doors closed to the past and being able to renew my mind daily!" —K.T.

―――⇒•◦⇐―――

"The Lord has freed me from my addiction to drugs. I was able to do that through leaning on Jesus for the strength. I needed to remain free and clean. I'd been an addict for 30 years. I had tried everything to get clean from addiction: rehab, moving away, doctors, medication. Nothing worked until Jesus.

"By closing the open door to drugs in my life and retraining my thoughts through His Word, and for me, memorizing scriptures I was able to overcome my addiction. The first scripture I memorized was 'I can do all things through Christ who strengthens me' (Philippians 4:13). It stood out to me and is one of my favorites. I know I can do nothing without Him, but with Him, and through Him, relying on Him, and His strength. I have remained free and clean now for 12 years!" —R.S.

―――⇒•◦⇐―――

"I started going to counseling because I was in the process of going through a divorce. I knew the Lord had plans for me to be a wife and mom, which meant I needed a complete healing over my life.

"I learned how to rely on the Lord through my grief and healing. Learning how to close spiritual doors and ending generational curses gave me so much peace and awareness. I now know how to protect my children, household, marriage, mind, spirit, and most importantly, my relationship with Christ. These are things I could have never learned on my own. I am so thankful for a God that had big plans for someone like me." —C.E.

RECOMMENDED RESOURCES

Recommended Bible Reading

- The Bible
- The Book of Proverbs: Wisdom for daily living. One chapter per day to correspond with the day of the month.
- Colossians, chapter 3
- Galatians, chapters 5 and 6
- Ephesians, chapters 4 and 5
- Matthew, chapters 4, 5, 6 and 7
- James, The book of
- John, chapter 15
- Psalm 119
- Romans, chapter 8 and 12
- 1 Corinthians, chapters 12 and 13
- 1 Peter 3:8-9
- Zondervan's *Life in the Spirit Study Bible*

Recommended Resources

- *My Heart—Christ's Home*, by Robert Boyd Munger, InterVarsity Press
- *Steps to Peace with God*, from the Billy Graham Evangelistic Association.
- *The Bride and the Church Booklet*, by Rev. Sandra Querin, available from abbasheart.com
- *The Freedom Booklet*, by Rev. Sandra Querin, available from abbasheart.com
- *Standards to Live By—Daily Bible Reading Guide*, available from abbasheart.com
- *Spiritual Body Builders Booklet*, available from abbasheart.com
- *Out of the Abyss—Victory from Deception*, sermon podcast by Rev. Sandra Querin available at abbasheart.com

- Bible Gateway—biblegateway.com
- Focus on the Family—focusonthefamily.com
- Caryn's Podcast: Foundations of Faith, available from abbas-heart.com. Click on the Resources button, then on Foundations of Faith.
    1. "Salvation, Assurance of Salvation, The Lordship of Jesus Christ"
    2. "Prayer, the Holy Spirit, and The Baptism of the Holy Spirit"
    3. "The Bible"
    4. "Closing Doors/Living an Overcoming Christian Life."

Suggested Books

- *Self-Confrontation—A Manual for In-Depth Biblical Discipleship*, from the Biblical Counseling Foundation, bcf.ministries.org
- *The Dynamics of Spiritual Warfare*, by Rev. Sandra Querin (soon to be released)
- *The Prayer of Job*, by Rev. Sandra Querin
- *The Prayer of Moses*, by Rev. Sandra Querin
- *The Christ Culture*, by Keith Carroll
- *Five to Thrive*, by Dr. Kathy Koch
- *Out of Control and Loving It*, by Lisa Bevere
- *Death to Self, the Path to Change and the Power of God*, by Guillermo Maldonado
- *A Shepherd Looks at Psalm 23*, by W. Phillip Keller
- *Zondervan's Pictorial Bible Dictionary*

Acknowledgments

Grecia Enns of Daisies and the Roses Calligraphy for all of her wonderful illustrations for this book.
Email: Grecia.enns@gmail.com
Instagram: @daisiesandtheroses

Much appreciation and thankfulness also go to my daughter-in-law, Megan Kilgore, Vivien Cooley, and Sandra Querin for their help and encouragement with this book.

Appendix

DISCIPLESHIP QUIZ

Discipleship is a process which enables you to "grow up" in the Lord Jesus Christ and equips you to overcome joyfully the pressures and trials of this present life based on Luke 9:23-24 and James 1:2-4. Discipleship requires constant self-examination that is in accordance with God's Word, based on Matthew 7:1-5, 1 Corinthians 11:31, and Galatians 6:4.

The following will help you evaluate your faithfulness as a disciple of Christ. For each question, rate yourself on a scale of 0—no faithfulness, complete self-centeredness to 10—perfect faithfulness, total Christ-centeredness.

Regardless of your present level of faithfulness, remember that God will help you make the necessary changes to be conformed to the image of His Son (see Romans 8:29; 2 Corinthians 3:18; Philippians 1:6). All of the characteristics of discipleship mentioned below are covered during this course. Biblical steps by which these characteristics can be incorporated into your life will also be explained.

1. Are you diligent in learning to handle accurately the Word of God? 2 Timothy 2:15.
2. Do you consistently examine yourself in light of God's Word instead of comparing yourself with the lives or expectations of others? 1 Samuel 16:7; Isaiah 55:8-11; Romans 3:23; 2 Corinthians 10:12; Hebrews 4:12.
3. Are you a doer of the Word? Being a doer of the Word requires continual hearing of God's Word and walking in it to receive the blessings of the Lord. Deuteronomy 11:26-28; Romans 10:17; Hebrews 5:14; James 1:22-25. The Word is completely

adequate for every area of life as it teaches, reproves, corrects, trains, and equips you in order that you may mature in Christ. 2 Timothy 3:16-17.

4. Do you deny yourself by putting off your natural self-centered-ness to follow the Lord Jesus Christ? Matthew 10:38-39; Luke 9:23-24.

5. Do you seek to please God in all things? John 8:29; 2 Corinthians 5:9; Ephesians 6:6-7; Colossians 1:10; 1 Thessalonians 2:4, 4:1; Hebrews 13:21; 1 John 3:22.

6. Are you a person of prayer? Continual prayer, with thanks-giving, leads to God's peace guarding your heart and mind in Christ Jesus. Philippians 4:6-7; 1 Thessalonians 5:17-18.

7. Do you place the welfare of others ahead of your own, thus fol-lowing the example of the Lord Jesus Christ? Matthew 20:25-28; Romans 15:1-3; Philippians 2:3-8.

8. Do you love others in biblical ways? 1 Corinthians 13:4-8a. By loving in this manner, you will follow the example of our Lord Jesus Christ and become known as His disciple. John 13:34-35, 15:12-13.

9. Are you faithfully using your spiritual gift(s) for God's glory and for the benefit of others? Romans 12:3-8; Ephesians 4:1-16; 1 Peter 4:10-11.

10. Do you regularly worship the Lord, remaining in fellowship and in ministry with other believers? Psalm 29:1-2, 122:1; John 4:23-24; Hebrews 10:24-25; 1 Peter 2:5; 1 John 1:7.

11. Are you ready at all times to give testimony for the hope that is within you, 1 Peter 3:15, giving glory to the Lord with your life, Matthew 5:16, seeking to reconcile others to God, and discipling them to walk in His way? Matthew 28:19-20; 2 Corinthians 5:18-20.

This portion is excerpted with permission from the Biblical Counseling Foundation's Self-Confrontation Manual (1991 Edition).

About the Author

First and foremost, CARYN KILGORE is a Christian and follower of Jesus Christ. She has been married to her wonderful husband, Allen, for more than four decades. She is the mother of Brent, a teacher; and Gregory, a pastor; and mother-in-law to Megan, a teacher. The loves of her life are her grandchildren.

Her hobbies include gardening, reading, and baking. She has been a biblical counselor for over 25 years and leads a team of men and women counselors at her church. Those teams do biblical counseling for men, women, children, and couples.

Caryn has a passion for and has had the privilege of leading hundreds of people to the Lord. She has done this through teaching, leading ladies retreats, discipling, and counseling. She was even privileged to be a counselor at a Billy Graham Crusade.

Caryn's calling in life is to equip people to walk in their callings and reach their full potential in Jesus Christ. She does this through teaching, counseling, and prayer.

Caryn's Life Verse:

And we pray this in order that you may live a life worthy of the Lord and please Him in every way: Bearing fruit in every good work and growing in the knowledge of God. Colossians 1:10

Contact Information:

You may order additional books through the Abba's Heart Ministry website: www.abbasheart.com
Or call the ministry office at: (559) 897-9575
Or email Caryn at: Caryn@abbasheart.com
Or through: Christianbook.com, Amazon, Barnes and Noble, or Kindle